*Pollution and the Death of Man:*
*The Christian View of Ecology*

D1440028

*By the same author*

ESCAPE FROM REASON (*Inter-Varsity Press*)
THE GOD WHO IS THERE
DEATH IN THE CITY (*Inter-Varsity Press*)
THE CHURCH AT THE END OF THE
  20th CENTURY (*Norfolk Press*)

# Pollution
## and the
## Death of Man:
## The Christian View of Ecology

by

FRANCIS A. SCHAEFFER

HODDER AND STOUGHTON
LONDON SYDNEY AUCKLAND TORONTO

# CONTENTS

# ACKNOWLEDGEMENTS

The article in Appendix I, 'The Historical Roots of Our Ecologic Crisis' by Lynn White, Jr., is reprinted with permission from *Science Magazine*, issue of March 10, 1967.

The article in Appendix II, 'Why Worry About Nature?' by Richard L. Means, copyright © 1967 by the *Saturday Review, Inc.*, is reprinted with permission from the *Saturday Review*.

# Chapter 1

## 'What have they done to our Fair Sister?'

Some time ago I was in Bermuda for a lecture, and I was invited by a young man internationally known in the area of ecology to visit his work. His name is David B. Wingate. He is especially known for his work in trying to save the cahow bird from extinction. The cahow bird is a little larger than a pigeon. It's almost extinct, and only breeds on a very few islands immediately around Bermuda, just off the main island. Wingate had struggled for several years to try to increase the number of the birds.

For many, many years people thought they were extinct. They are not, but they are rapidly moving towards it and Wingate's aim is to breed these birds up to a higher number again.

As we went around visiting the nests, we were talking together about the whole problem of ecology. Arising out of this, he told me that he was beginning to lose ground in his battle because the chicks were not hatching any longer in the same proportion as they had previously. If they had continued to hatch in the same proportion he would have been well on his way to success. But instead of this, he found that they were hatching less and less. An embryo chick was taken out of the egg and dissected. They found that its tissues were filled with D.D.T. Wingate was convinced that here was the reason why they were no longer hatching in the same number.

Now, the startling thing about this is that the cahow is a sea-feeding bird; it doesn't feed anywhere near land—it only feeds in the middle of the ocean. So it was obvious that it was getting its D.D.T. not close to shore but out in the middle of the Atlantic Ocean, or almost in the

7

middle of the Atlantic Ocean. In other words, the use of D.D.T. on land is also polluting the whole sea. It is coming down through the rivers out into the ocean, and in the ocean birds like these are eating it and are dying off simply because D.D.T. has been carried into the middle of the Atlantic Ocean.[1]

When Thor Heyerdahl crossed the Atlantic recently in a papyrus boat he pointed out that previously when they had travelled in the Kon-Tiki in mid-ocean they had been able to use the ocean water quite freely, but on this present trip almost all the way across the ocean there was nothing but rubbish.

So here is the problem. A man in California points this up vividly. He has arranged a tombstone down by the ocean, and on it he has carved this epitaph: 'The Oceans born—the Lord gave' (he gives a hypothetical date, and then) 'Died, A.D. 1979—Man hath taken away, Cursed be the Name of Man.'

The simple fact is that if man is not able to solve his ecological problems, then man's resources are going to die. Already we have what are called the 'red floods' coming in, red tides caused by the upset of the ecological balance of the oceans. It is quite conceivable that man will soon no longer be able to fish the oceans in the way he has fished there in the past, and if the balance of the oceans is changed too much, that man will even find himself without enough oxygen to breathe.

So the whole problem of ecology is dumped on this generation's neck. Ecology means 'the study of the balance of living things in nature'. But as the word is being currently used, it means not only that but also the problem of the destruction man has brought upon nature. It is related to such factors as water pollution, destructive noise-levels and air pollution in the great cities of the world. We are reading and hearing of this on

[1] For a technical study of Wingate's work, see *Science Magazine*, March 1, 1968, pp. 979–81.

every side and from all over the world. For example, *Newsweek* had an article on 'The Dilemma of Tokyo', where you have to go in and pay a certain amount—up to about two shillings—in order to get breaths of oxygen from machines. Just as you buy a cup of coffee, so you pay for a few breaths of oxygen in the middle of Tokyo at its worst times of pollution.

Darwin, when close to dying, acknowledged several times in his writings that two things had become dull to him as he got older, on the basis of his own theory. The first one was that he had lost his joy in the arts; and secondly, that he had lost his joy in nature. This is very intriguing. Darwin put out his proposition that nature, including man, is based only on the impersonal plus time plus chance, and he has to acknowledge at the end of his life that it had had these adverse effects on him. I believe what we are seeing today is the same effect on our total culture as on Darwin personally : first of all in the area of the arts; then, secondly, in the area of nature. The distressing thing about this is that orthodox Christians often really have had no better sense in this area than unbelievers. The death of 'joy' in nature is leading to the death of nature itself.

This sort of anxiety is even being expressed in the area of 'pop' music. The Doors have a song called 'Strange Days' in which they say :

> What have they done to the earth,
> What have they done to our fair sister
> Ravaged and plundered,
> And ripped her and bit her,
> Stuck her with knives in the side of the dawn
> And tied her with fences and dragged her down[2]

At any rate, people everywhere are now beginning to

[2] From 'Strange Days' by The Doors. Elektra EKS 74014. Copyright Doors Music Company.

discuss what can be done about it. An intriguing article by Lynn White, Jr., and 'The Historical Roots of Our Ecologic Crisis' was published in *Science Magazine* (March 19, 1967). White is a professor of History at the University of California, Los Angeles.

In his article he argued that the crisis in ecology is Christianity's fault. It is a brilliant article, in which he argues that although we no longer are a Christian world, but a post-Christian one, nevertheless we still retain a Christian mentality in the area of ecology. He says Christianity had a bad view of nature, and so this is carried over into the present-day post-Christian world. He bases his allegations of a 'bad view of nature' on the fact that Christianity taught that man had dominion over nature and so man has treated nature in a destructive way. He does see that there is no solution to ecological problems—any more than there is to sociological problems—without a 'base'. The base of man's thinking must change.

Modern man's viewpoint, in the post-Christian world (as I have dealt with it in my previous books) is without any categories, and without any base upon which to build. Lynn White understands the need of a base in the area of ecology. To quote from him 'What people do about their ecology depends on what they think about themselves in relation to things around them. Human ecology is deeply conditioned by beliefs about our nature and our destiny—that is by religion.' Here I believe he is completely right. Men *do* what they *think*. Whatever their world view is, this is the thing which will spill over into the external world. This is true in every area, in student revolt and sociology, in all science and technology, as well as in the area of ecology.

White's solution is to ask, 'Why don't we go back to St. Francis of Assisi?' And he contrasts St. Francis with what he sees as the 'orthodox view' of men having the 'right' to despoil nature. 'The great spiritual revolutionary

10

in western history, St. Francis, proposed what he thought to be an alternative Christian view of nature in men's relationship to it . . .'

Now the traditional view, according to Lynn White, is that because Christianity said 'man has dominion' it follows that man can despoil and exploit nature without limit. According to White, St. Francis put forth an alternative Christian view of nature and man's relationship to it: 'he tried to substitute the idea of the equality of all creatures, including man, for the idea of man's limitless rule of creation'.

Both our present science and our present technology, according to White, are so tinctured with orthodox Christian arrogance towards nature that no solution for our problem of ecology can be expected from them alone. He says that technology is not going to solve the problem because it is powered with its view of dominion over nature, which equals limitless exploitation. 'Since the roots of our trouble are so largely religious, the remedy must also be essentially religious, whether we call it that or not. We must re-think and re-feel our nature and destiny. The profoundly religious but heretical sense of the primitive Franciscans, for the spiritual autonomy of all parts of nature, may point out a direction. I propose Francis as the patron saint for ecology.'

The discussion of this was picked up and carried further, and aroused a great deal of interest. In the *Saturday Review* of December 2, 1967, Richard Means, who is Associate Professor of Sociology at the College of Kalamazoo, Michigan, quoted White and extended White's concept and asked: Why not give a pantheistic solution to this? Why not begin to find a solution to this in the direction of pantheism? In fact, he ties this call for a solution based on pantheism into what he calls the 'cool cats' of the modern generation in their interest in Zen Buddhism. He is saying here, 'Wouldn't it be a solution

11

if we just said, "We're all of one essence." '

So here pantheism is proposed as an answer to our ecological dilemma. But is it an answer at all? That is a question we must now turn to consider.

# Chapter 2

## Pantheism: Man is no more than the Grass

The dictionary definition of ecology as 'biology, dealing with the interrelations between organisms and their environment' allows for two types of considerations. First, the interrelationship of organisms, and secondly, the interrelationship of organisms and their environment. This latter has suddenly become especially important, and now the word 'ecology' is being used in a way which puts an emphasis on the problem of the balance of nature and man's modern destruction of the balance of nature. It comes from the realisation that man is destroying the balance of nature, and that raises the question of what to do about it in detail, and upon what base something constructive can be done.

'Why not try to find a solution to this in the direction of God returning to pantheism?' This is the question asked by Richard Means in his important *Saturday Review* article. So here we find a use of the concept of pantheism by a Western scientist, a sociologist, in his effort to solve modern man's problem in relationship to the saving of nature, i.e. the ecological problem. This man seems to be trying to use pantheism in a very specific way, however, not as a real, religious answer at all, but merely in a sociological or a scientific pragmatic usage of pantheism.

The article is entitled 'Why worry About Nature?' Means begins the article by quoting Albert Schweitzer: 'The great fault of all ethics hitherto has been that they believed themselves to have to deal only with the relation of man to man.' He thus quotes Schweitzer as saying ecology is a problem of ethics, but that man's only concept of ethics has been 'man to man'. A little bit further on we find Means saying, 'The notion that man's relation to nature is a moral one finds very few articulate champions, even among contemporary religious writers.' He is proposing, then, that man's relationship to nature is moral, but he says that not many theologians have dealt with this, not even modern theologians. He proceeds to refer to Harvey Cox's book, *The Secular City*. Cox, of course, is a very liberal theologian, a proponent of the 'God is dead' theology. Means says that even with Cox 'The city is taken for granted and the moral dimensions of (Cox's) analysis are limited to man's relations to man within this urban world, and not with the animals, the plants, the trees, and the air—that is, the natural habitat.' Cox and the modern theology have not dealt with this problem, but it should be remembered that much modern theology is in the direction of pantheism and thus Means' suggestion of a pragmatic pantheistic base for solving our ecological problems fits naturally into the prevalent climate stretching all the way from the 'rock' groups to the theological faculties.

Means goes on to refer, interestingly enough, to Eric Hoffer, who is a popular American folk philosopher. He is a longshoreman who says many really profound things and has become very, very popular indeed with the intellectuals, as well as being invited to the White House, and so on. 'Eric Hoffer, one of the few contemporary social critics who have met head-on the issue of man's relationship to nature, has warned in these pages of the danger of romanticising nature' ('A strategy for the War with Nature' in the *Saturday Review*, February 5, 1966). Hoffer, Means points out, has already warned us against romanticising our relationship to nature. Romanticising means that one looks at nature and projects into it man's reaction. So one would look at a cat and one would think of it as though it were reacting the way a man reacts. Hoffer warns (and very properly) against this. However, his solution (according to Means) ends like this: 'The great accomplishment of man is to transcend nature, to separate himself from the demands of instinct. Thus, according to Hoffer, a fundamental characteristic of man is to be found in his capacity to free himself from the restrictions of the physical and the biological.' In other words, Hoffer is really not proposing that we should come to terms with nature. Not as far as Means understands him, anyway. What Hoffer is saying is that man has to transcend nature, that is, he has to get on top of the physical and the biological instincts in himself.

It should be said that it is correct to reject the romanticising of nature as an answer or a solution. Firstly, nature, as it now is, is not always benevolent; and secondly, to project our feelings and thoughts into a tree would mean that we would have no base upon which to justify cutting down and using the tree as a shelter for man.

Those who are familiar with Koestler's *The Man and the Machine* will recognise Hoffer's ideas to be merely a more poetic form of his concept. Koestler, along with Adler (*The Difference in Man and the Difference it Makes*) and Michael Polanyi of Oxford stand together, attacking the classical view of evolution, at least pragmatically—they are united at least in saying that it is leading us in the wrong direction. But Koestler in *The Man and the Machine* comes up with the final solution by pleading with science to make a pill to bring together the upper and the lower brain. For Koestler the lower brain deals with the instincts and the emotions and the upper brain deals with the intellect and reasoning—according to Koestler the real problem lies in the separation of the two. The point to be made here is that Hoffer's idea of man's 'getting on top of' his nature in order to free himself from the restrictions of the physical and the biological, is, interestingly enough, in the direction of Koestler's concept.

Reverting to Means' article, he goes on to ask, and answer, an important question. Remembering that he is proposing the thesis that man's relationship to nature is a moral, and not just a scientific crisis, his question and his immediate answer provide a brilliant snapshot of modern man: 'What, then, is the moral crisis? It is, I think, a pragmatic problem.'

Here is a remarkable combination of phrases being put together; the moral dissolved into the pragmatic. He starts off with a moral crisis but suddenly all one is left with is a pragmatic problem—'It involves the actual social consequences of myriad and unconnected acts. The crisis comes by combining the results of a mistreatment of our environment. It involves the negligence of a small businessman on the Kalamazoo River, the irresponsibility of a large co-operation on Lake Erie, the impatient use of insecticides by a farmer in California, the stripping of land by Kentucky mine operators. Unfortunately, there is a long history of unnecessary and tragic destruction of animal and natural resources on the face of this continent.' Of course the pressure becomes greater on a world scale, and he is, of course, right in pointing out that there is a serious problem. But that does not change his problem of dealing with the problem! He wants a moral base with which to deal with the ecological problem, but soon all he has is the word 'moral'. And all he is left with is the pragmatic and technological.

As one faces the population explosion the ecological problem becomes even greater, nowhere more so than in Switzerland. All one has to think of is beautiful Lac Leman and the difference since we came to Switzerland almost twenty-one years ago—a major difference. The lake is not only lower but it is not even the same lake. If the population explosion goes on, what is to be done about Lac Leman, as well as the Kalamazoo River. As the pressure gets greater, upon what basis—different from the one we have employed in the past—are we to

16

treat the nature which is our environment and upon which our life in this world depends? As the Sierra Club calendar for 1970 puts it, 'The moon, Mars, Saturn . . . nice places to visit, but you wouldn't want to live there.' Human life—in this present life, that is—depends on the uniquely balanced environment of this world.

Means goes on to talk about the passenger pigeons, of which there were once many, in the United States, but they are now extinct. The same can be said about the seal industry. 'The trouble is, however, we do not seem to learn very much from these sad happenings for (to the anguish of men who have thrilled to the images created by Herman Melville and the great white whale) such marine scientists as Scott McVay believe that commercial fishing is endangering the whale, the last abundant species in the world. For those more inclined towards the cash nexus there goes a profitable industry.' He continues that it is not only an economic loss, but that 'those of us who have a respect for nature—in particular, for our mammalian kinsmen—the death of these great creatures will leave a void in God's creation and in the imagination of men for generations to come'. The use of Means' phrase 'in God's creation', which for many Christians would inspire hope as to the kind of answer he might give us, must not be misunderstood, as I will point out later.

Then Means touches on other basic issues, referring to the mighty Hudson River, the Great Lakes and the state of the air we breathe. Because of these matters, and hundreds like them, we can see why men are wrestling, in a way that they have never wrestled before, with the problem of ecology. So there is a true dilemma. Modern man has seen that we are upsetting the balance of nature and the problem is drastic and urgent. It is not just a matter of aesthetics, nor is the problem only future—the *quality* of life has already diminished for most modern men. For the future, many thinking men see the ecological threat as greater than that of all-out nuclear warfare.

Means proceeds to offer his solutions to this dilemma. These are presented as first a negative, and then later a positive side. It is worth considering Means' thinking in detail, because it is representative of what, with various modifications, we are hearing from a multitude of sources —and will be hearing more and more in the next few years. Indeed, Aldous Huxley, in his last novel, *Island*,[1] pictures a 'utopian' future in which the first lessons given to schoolchildren will be in ecology. He then goes on to observe: 'Elementary ecology leads straight to elementary Buddhism.' I have recently been lecturing at Buck Hill Falls, Pennsylvania, and another conference there at the same time was called 'The Conference on Environment and Population'. After a light show presenting the modern problems of ecology, the answer was set forth that the solution must be in the direction of pantheism. We are going to hear much of this in the immediate future. Pantheism will be pressed as the only answer to ecological problems and will be one more influence in the West becoming increasingly East in its thinking.

What is man's relation to nature? 'Why is man's relation to nature a moral crisis? It is a moral crisis because it is a historical one involving man's history and culture, expressed at its roots by our religious and ethical views of nature—which have been relatively unquestioned in this context.' Up to this point one can agree with his diagnosis. But then he goes on to make a negative statement: 'The historian in medieval culture, Lynn White, Jr., brilliantly traced the origin and consequences of this expression in an insightful article in *Science* last March: "The Historical Roots of Our Ecologic Crisis." He argues that the Christian notion of a transcendent God, removed from nature and breaking into nature only through revelation, removed spirit from nature and

[1] *Island*, by Aldous Huxley. Penguin edition, pp. 219, 220.

18

allows, in an ideological sense, for an easy exploitation of nature.

'On the American scene the Calvinistic and the deistic concepts of God were peculiarly alike at this point. Both envisioned God as absolutely transcendent, apart from the world, isolated from nature and organic life. As to the contemporary implications of this dichotomy between spirit and nature Professor White says ". . . To a Christian a tree can be no more than a physical fact. The whole concept of the sacred grove is alien to Christianity and to the ethos of the West. For nearly two millennia Christian missionaries have been chopping down sacred groves, which are idolatrous because they assume spirit in nature." '

Means' first answer, according to his quotation, must be found in his proposition that our ecological problem exists because of Christianity. So Means' 'negative' answer to his question is to lay the blame squarely on Christianity as such, which has, in its intrinsic nature, on his premise, created and sustained the ecological problem.

In contrast to this, we may agree with the first part of the next paragraph in Means' article. 'Perhaps, as Lynn White suggests, the persistence of this as a moral problem is illustrated in the protest of the contemporary generation of beats and hippies.'

Our agreement with Means at this point centres on the fact that the hippies did understand something. They are right in fighting the plastic culture, and the Church should have been fighting it too, a long, long time ago, before the hippies ever hove into view. More than this, the hippies are right in the fact that part of the plastic culture—modern man, the mechanistic world-view in university textbooks and in practice, the total threat of the machine, the establishment technology, the bourgeois upper-middle-class mentality—*is* poor in its sensitivity to nature. This is totally right. The hippies are right in saying that both the bourgeois upper-middle-class mentality and modern technology have little sensitivity for nature. As a utopian group the hippies understand something very real, both as to the culture as a culture, but also as to the poverty of modern man's concept of nature and the way the machine is eating up nature on every side. At this point I would side with the hippies.

However, Means carries on and suggests that the hippies have perhaps a good solution. We may differ with him here, but undoubtedly he does understand what the hippies' solution is. He says: 'There may be a "sound instinct" involved in the fact that some of these so-called beats have turned to Zen Buddism. It may represent an overdue perception of the fact that we need to appreciate more fully the religious and moral dimensions of the relation between nature and the human spirit.' This shows a quite proper discernment of the hippy direction, which is towards pantheism. He would not need to limit it to Zen because it is pantheism in general. Thus, after having given a negative statement in saying that for the solution we must get rid of Christianity, in its place we have a suggested solution in the direction of the total drift of our culture. For, as I have said, almost all the new theologians are drifting towards pantheism in company with the hippies, the Beatles in their middle period and many of the 'pop' prophets. Indeed, much of the surrounding culture undoubtedly is moving in the direction of the West becoming the East. And Means offers this solution with regard to the problem of ecology. This is undoubtedly why he quoted Schweitzer in the first sentence of his article. At the end of his life Schweitzer was a pantheist, laying great emphasis on 'reverence for life', by which he meant that all that is, is of one essence. Means starts with Schweitzer as a man well known in the West but who was a pantheist.

This is why I questioned Means' statement about 'God's creation'. He is really using a Western term for a completely different concept. The term 'God's creation' has no real place in pantheistic thinking. To speak of 'God's creation' in reference to the pantheistic system is meaningless, for everything is an extension of the essence of God. One simply does not have a *creation* but only an extension of God's essence, in which any such term as 'God's creation'—as though He were a personal God who created, whose creation was external to Himself (all of which is wrapped up in our Western phrase 'God's creation')—has no place.

It is clear that he is talking about a real pantheism when Means goes on: 'On the other hand, the refusal to connect the human spirit to nature may reflect the traditional thought-patterns of Western society wherein nature is conceived to be a separate substance—a material—mechanical, and, in a metaphysical sense, irrelevant to man.' What he's trying to do is link up the fact that all that is, is the same substance with nature: and in this way to get a sort of reverence for nature that will cause us to treat nature more gently.

He says towards the end of the article: 'Such a view should help destroy egoistic, status politics, for it helps unmask the fact that other men's activities are not just private, inconsequential and limited in themselves; their acts, mediated through changes in nature, affect my life, my children, and the generations to come.'

What is interesting here is to see—as noted earlier—that his use of the word 'moral' only leaves us with the pragmatic. The only reason we are called upon to treat nature well is because of its effects on man, and my children and the generation to come. So in reality, in spite of all Means' words, man is left with a completely egoistic position in regard to nature. No reason is given—moral or logical—for regarding nature as something in itself. We are left with a purely pragmatic issue.

Means ends his article: '. . . Our contemporary moral crisis, then, goes much deeper than questions of political power and law, of urban riots and slums. It may, at least in part, reflect American society's almost utter disregard for the value of nature.' Here we must agree with him. We have mistreated nature—not just the Americans, but other people as well throughout the world.

But notice, he gives no answer; and the 'no-answer' falls into three different levels. First of all, the moral only equals the pragmatic, and this, of course, is related to the fact that a modern man in this position has no basis for morals because he has no absolutes to which he can appeal. One can have a basis for something else—a social contract, a hedonism—but one can never have morals without absolutes. We may call them morals, but it always ends up as 'I like', or social contract, neither of which are morals. The latter is a majority vote, or the arbitrary absolutes of an élite in society. And having no absolutes modern man has no categories. One can think of the movie *Blow-Up*: 'murder without guilt; love without meaning'. One cannot have real answers without categories, and these men have no categories beyond pragmatic technological ones.

This can be seen in Means' article when he talks about cutting down the sacred groves. He has no categories whereby we could cut down a sacred grove when it is an idol and yet not be against trees as trees. As far as he is concerned, these categories do not exist. For him the fact that a Christian would cut down a sacred grove when it has become an idol proves that Christians are against trees. It is rather like arguing concerning the Bible and art. The Bible is not 'against' art. But supposing somebody argued that the Jews broke the brazen serpent which Moses had made (2 Kings 18:4). Here one has a serpent made of brass which the godly king broke, so therefore God is 'against' art. Of course, from the biblical viewpoint, it is not a statement against art at all. They were against the brazen serpent, which God had originally commanded to be made, *only when it became an idol*. God commanded this work of art to be made, but when it became an idol it was to be destroyed. The reason was not that the Bible is against art but because the work of art had become an idol. This means that one has categories.

In contrast, this man—modern man—has no categories. This brings us back to the first point. The moral only equals the pragmatic on a very crude level, in spite of all this nice terminology. So we must not think that Means is a man giving us a moral answer, a high answer; he is not. It is a very low answer indeed.[2]

The second thing is that Means uses these religious words ('moral' for 'pragmatic') over and over again as religious connotation words for the purpose of motivation. He is also using the word 'pantheism' as a motivation word. This is something we must always be careful of. Words have two meanings, the definition and the connotation. The connotation goes on no matter what you do with the definition. Modern man smashes the definition of religious words but nevertheless likes to cash in on their connotation/motivation force. And this is precisely what Means is doing here. By using these words he hopes (even though he has indicated in his definition 'moral' equals 'pragmatic') that people will treat nature a little better because of the religious connotations of the words. It is one more illustration of something that is about us on every side.

The third thing to notice is that what one has here is

[2] The use of the *terms* moral or ethical to equal only the pragmatic in relationships to ecology is clearly seen in Frank Fraser Darling's 1969 Reith Lectures. He, too, says we need a moral or ethical base if the problems of ecology are to be solved, but ends with no moral or ethical base but only a crude pragmatism. For Darling, nature as such is given no rights, man is all. There is no ethical base in regard to nature as a thing in itself. Like Means, all that is left is man and man's children. Note especially the conclusion of the last Reith Lecture as recorded in *The Listener* of December 18, 1969.

sociological religion and sociological science. It is important to note that Means is a sociologist. One does not have religion as religion; not does one have science as science. What one has is both religion and science being used and manipulated for sociological purposes.

Edmund Leach, the Cambridge anthropologist, in an article in the *New York Review of Books* (February 1966), very clearly chooses a scientific solution, not because it has anything to do with objective science but because it leads to the sociological answer that he wants. Edmund Leach is at this place the very opposite of a scientist. Here is no scientist as a scientist: here is a scientist using science for sociological manipulation. With this, then, a parallel can be found between Edmund Leach in his article and Richard Means in his. The latter is also using science and religion for purely sociological ends. With it, science dies, religion dies, and all you are left with is sociological manipulation.

Remember what I have emphasised before—it is worth considering this article by Richard Means in detail because the thoughts presented in this article are representative of those which are, and will be, sounded by many voices, with a multitude of variations and subtleties, in the next few years. This is true about the theoretical and practical discussions in general, and also the ecological discussion of the relationship of man to nature in particular. And the same basic factors are involved whether the unity of everything that is is expressed with some form of the religious connotation word 'pantheism', or with purely secular terms, in reducing everything to energy particles.

Let us examine the reasons why pantheism in any form does not give a sufficient answer. Pantheism eventually gives no meaning to any particulars. In true pantheism unity has meaning, but the particulars have no meaning, including the particular of man. Also, if the particulars have no meaning, then nature has no meaning, including the particular of man. A meaning to particulars does not exist philosophically in any pantheistic system, whether it is the pantheism of the East or the 'pan-everything-ism' of beginning only with the energy particles, in the modern West. In both cases, eventually the particulars have no meaning. One is left only with Jean-Paul Sartre's absurd universe. Pantheism gives you an answer for unity, but it gives no meaning to the diversity. Pantheism is not an answer.

This is not just a theoretical dilemma—that the particulars have no meaning in pantheism. It is not just a vague philosophical objection. It leads to important conclusions. First, any 'results' one does get from pantheism are obtained only by projecting *man's* feelings into *nature*. And that is simply Hoffer's romanticism; an endowing of the lower with a human reaction. So when we see a chicken, we endow its love-life with human qualities. But that is to evade the *reality* of the chicken. This kind of an answer can only get any result from these motivation words by projecting into nature human feelings. This is the romanticism that Hoffer properly rejects.

What I am saying is that a pantheistic answer is not just a theoretically weak answer but it is also a weak answer in *practice*. A man who begins to take a pantheistic view towards nature has no answer for the fact that nature has two faces; it has a benevolent face, but it is also an enemy over and over again. Nature is viewed as normal, by the pantheist. There is no place for abnormality in nature. This becomes a very practical dilemma in Camus' *Plague* (*La Peste*) where Camus comments on the dilemma facing Orion the ratcatcher: well, if he joins with the doctors and fights the plague, he is fighting against God, or if he joins with the priest and does not fight God by not fighting the plague, he is not being humanitarian. Camus never resolves this problem. If we accept this romantic and non-Christian mysticism, the difficulty is that we have no solution for the fact that nature is often not benevolent.

If everything is one, and a part of the essence with no basic distinction, how does one explain nature when it is destructive? What is the theoretical answer? As Camus understood, it isn't just a theoretical problem. Rather, how do I fight the plague?

The Christian *can* fight it. When Christ stood in front of the tomb of Lazarus (John 11), He was claiming to be divine and yet He was furious (and the Greek makes it plain that He was *furious*). He could be furious with the plague *without being angry with Himself*. This turns upon the historic, space–time Fall. Consequently, the Christian does not have Camus' difficulty. But if one is putting forth a pantheistic, mystical answer, there is no answer to the fact that nature is not always benevolent, and one has no way to understand the origin of this double face of nature, one has no real way to 'fight the plague'. There may be much high-sounding talk, but eventually this is true of all pantheism, either Eastern or modern Western—either hippie or modern theologian.

Again, a pantheistic stand always brings man to an impersonal and low place rather than elevating him. This is an absolute rule. Whether the pantheistic answer is the modern scientism, related back to the energy particle, or whether it is Eastern, eventually nature does not become high but man becomes low. This can be seen over and over again. Schweitzer spoke much of reverence for life, but a doctor who worked with him said that he wished Schweitzer had had less reverence for life and more love for it and for men. At the end of his life, Schweitzer's pantheism, instead of going towards a higher view of those among whom he worked, went towards a lower view.

The Eastern pantheism leads to this same thing. In the Eastern countries there is no real base for the dignity of man. Thus, it must be pointed out that *idealistic* Marxism could only have come as a Christian heresy: it could never have originated in the East. The strength of *idealistic* Marxism is its *talk* of the dignity of man. The East would never have produced this because there is no place for a genuine dignity of man in the pantheistic East. Idealistic Marxism is a Judeo-Christian heresy.

The same is true even of economics. The economic dilemma of India is complicated by the pantheistic system, in which the rats and the cows are allowed to eat up food that man needs. Instead of man being raised, in reality he is lowered. Rats and cows are finally given preference to man himself, and man begins to disappear into the woodwork in economics as well as in the area of personality, love and so on.[3]

When anyone begins to propose the pantheistic answer, he ignores the fact that far from raising nature eventually to man's height, pantheism will push both men and nature down together into a bog. Eventually there are no categories, and there is eventually no reason to distinguish bad nature from good nature. Pantheism leaves us with the Marquis de Sade's dictum, 'What is, is right' in morals, and man as no more than the grass.

[3] See 'Wilful Waste, Woeful Want', by Max Krischner, *The Listener*, January 26, 1967.

## Chapter 3

## Other Inadequate Answers

Pantheism is not the answer—as the West turns to pantheism to solve its ecological problems, the human will be even more decreased and pragmatic, impersonal technology will reign even more securely. But having said that, let us quickly add that a poor Christianity is not the answer, either. There is a 'Christianity' which gives no better answer than pantheism: Byzantine pre-Renaissance Christianity, for instance. The Byzantine represented that the only truly valuable thing is heavenly —so high, so lifted up, so holy that one did not ever make a real picture of Mary; the icons and mosaics are only symbols of her. The only thing that really mattered in life—in the Byzantine period—was the heavenly. These things are so far off that one does not even make a picture of them; one just makes symbols. This kind of Christianity will never give an answer to the problem of nature, for in this nature has no real importance. So there is indeed a form of Christianity that has no *proper* emphasis on nature.

At a certain point in history, as the medieval died and Renaissance man was born, suddenly Van Eyck began to paint nature. Likewise, in that marvellous Carmine chapel in Florence, Masaccio went beyond Giotto and began to paint nature as real nature. And at that point we could have gone towards a truly Christian art—because there is a real place for nature in true Christianity. Van Eyck and his backgrounds, and Masaccio painting in the round with the proper light and so on, could have gone either way—either towards a truly Christian art, in which nature had a proper place, or towards humanism.

Pantheism is no answer for a proper view of nature, but one must understand that just any kind of Christianity is no answer either; not a Byzantine Christianity, nor a Christianity based on a nature/grace situation. Neither will produce an answer. Nor is there any answer in the concept of nature and freedom held by Jean-Jacques Rousseau or Kant; nor in a Kierkegaardian kind of Christianity.[1] In all these areas one searches in vain for a Christian answer, or any real answer (even if Christian terms are used) and this includes any real answer for a proper view of nature.

But of course there exists a different kind of Christianity. The Christianity of the Reformation does give a unified answer, and this unity has meaning not only in heavenly things, but also in regard to nature. God has spoken. And because God has spoken, there is a unity. This gave the unity of the Reformation, in contrast to the nature/grace non-unity of the Renaissance. It turns upon the fact that God has spoken and told us something about both heavenly things and nature. On the basis of God's speaking, we know something truly of both universals and particulars, and this includes the meaning of the particulars and the proper use of the particulars. This unity has not come from a rationalism, a humanism, in which man is generating something out of himself, gathering and looking at the particulars and then trying to make a universal, whether it be a philosophic universal, or Leonardo da Vinci trying to paint the 'soul'.[2] The Reformation believed what the Bible says, that God has revealed truly about Himself and the *cosmos*, and that therefore there is a unity. The Westminster Confession of Faith—that marvellous statement of Christian doc-

[1] For a detailed consideration of these points, only touched on here, see *The God Who is There* (Hodder and Stoughton, 1968) and *Escape from Reason* (Inter-Varsity Press, 1968).
[2] These matters are also dealt with in detail in *The God Who is There* and *Escape from Reason*.

trine—says that God has revealed His attributes and these are true not only to us *but to Him*. So we have a true, but not exhaustive, knowledge, since God has spoken about Himself and about the *cosmos* and about history. This is the kind of Christianity that has an answer, including an answer about nature and man's relationship to it.

One feels this already in the paintings of Dürer, who in fact was painting a few years before Luther broke forth. As Professor Rookmaker of the Free University in Amsterdam points out, Dürer went through a humanistic period, and then he rejected the humanistic answer and came up with the biblical answer, and in that answer he knew what to do with nature.

One can also think of the post-Reformation Dutch painters, who painted nature beautifully and in its proper place. Without question, the greatest Dutch painting is that in which nature, the world as it is, had a tremendously important place. With Van Eyck in the North prior to the Reformation, and with Masaccio in the South, it did not go right: it went into humanism that came to a dead end in modern man, and modern man does not have any answer for nature either in his painting or his use of nature in life, just as he does not have any answer for man. But the Dutch painters after the Reformation were able to give nature its proper place, the Reformation having restored a *unity* on the basis of the revelation of God. Because they had a real unity which included heavenly things and nature, they had a real place for nature.

It is well to stress, then, that Christianity does not automatically have an answer: it has to be the right kind of Christianity, and there is a poor orthodox or evangelical Christianity that does not give any answer. Any Christianity that rests upon a dichotomy—some sort of Platonic concept—simply does not have an answer to nature, and we must say with tears that much orthodoxy, much evangelical Christianity is rooted in a Platonic concept wherein the only interest is in the 'upper story', in the heavenly things, in 'saving the soul' and only getting it to heaven. In this Platonic concept, even though orthodox and evangelical terminology is used, there is little or no interest in the proper pleasures of the body or the proper uses of the intellect. In such a Christianity there is a strong tendency to see nothing in nature beyond its use as one of the classic proofs of God's existence. 'Look at nature,' we are told, 'Look at the Alps. God must have made them.' And that is the end. Nature has become merely an academic proof of the existence of the Creator, with little value in itself. Christians of this outlook do not show an interest in nature *itself*. They use it simply as an apologetic weapon, rather than thinking or talking about the real value of nature.

An extreme example of this attitude can be found in what the Dutch Christians call 'The Black Stocking Calvinists' in Holland. These Black Stocking Calvinists have a tradition that they may treat their animals cruelly because the animals do not have a soul and are not going to heaven. Many of the Black Stocking people in Holland would say that they are very, very orthodox—but actually they are not orthodox. Theirs is Christianity in a perverted form. As far as credalism is concerned, they are very strong. But these people will actually beat and kick their animals, for the simple reason that the animals do not have a soul and are not going to heaven, so they can be treated in any way we wish. They have a sub-Christian view concerning nature.

One can find the same deficient concept in less extreme forms in many places. I was lecturing in a certain Christian school some years ago. Just across a ravine from this school there is what they call a 'hippie community' (though they aren't *real* hippies!). Across this ravine, on the other side, you see trees and some farms. Here, I was told, they had pagan grape stomps. Being in-

31

terested, I made my way across the ravine and met one of the leading men in this 'Bohemian' community.

We got on very well, as we talked of ecology and as I was able to speak of the Christian answer to life and ecology, and he paid me the compliment (and I accepted it as such) of telling me that I was the first person from 'across the ravine' who had ever been shown the place where they had their grape stomps, and the real pagan image they had there (the whole thing set against the classical background of Greece and Rome) which was the centre of the grape stomps.

Having shown me all this, he looked across to the Christian school and said to me, 'Look at that, isn't that ugly?' And it was! I could not refute him. It was an ugly building, without even trees around it. The thing was ugly!

It was then that I realised what a horrible situation this was. When I stood on Christian ground and looked at the Bohemian people's place, it was beautiful. (These people had even gone to the trouble of running their electricity cables under the level of the trees so that they couldn't be seen.) Then I stood on pagan ground and looked at the Christian community and saw ugliness. That is horrible.

Here you have a Christianity that is failing to take into account man's responsibility and man's proper relationship to nature.

So pantheism is not going to solve our international, ecological problem. St. Francis's concept, as presented by Lynn White, is not going to solve it—the concept that everything is equal and everything is spiritually autonomous. Because it is obvious in practice that man really does have a special and control role in nature that nothing else has. And thirdly, a Platonic view of Christianity is not going to solve it. Here Lynn White, unhappily, is right. He looks back over the history of Christianity and sees that there is too much Platonic thinking in Christianity where nature is concerned.

Now what is the genuine biblical view that *will* give a sufficient base for solving the ecological problem? What should be our attitude to and our treatment of nature? What is the biblical view of nature? Let us from now consider that question.

## Chapter 4

### The Christian View: Creation

The beginning of the Christian view of nature is the concept of Creation; that God was there before the beginning and God created everything out of nothing. From this, we must understand that Creation is not an extension of the essence of God. Created things have an existence in themselves. They are really there.

Whitehead, Oppenheimer and others have pointed out that modern science was only born out of a surrounding consensus of historic Christianity. Why? Because, as Whitehead has emphasised, Christianity believes that God has created an external world that is really there and because He is a reasonable God, one can expect to be able to find the order of the universe *by reason*. Whitehead is absolutely right about this. He is not a Christian, but he understands that there would never have been modern science without the biblical view of Christianity.

It is the same in the area of nature. It is the biblical view of nature that gives nature a value *in itself*: not to be used merely as a weapon or argument in apologetics, but of value in itself because God made it.

Jean-Paul Sartre states that the basic philosophic question is that something is there. And nature *is* there ... even if man doesn't know why. Christians know why it's there! Because God created it out of nothing, and it is in its place! Created things are not an extension of God's essence; they are not a 'dream of God', as some Eastern philosophies claim: they are really there. That may sound naïve and obvious, but it is not: it is a profound concept with profound consequences. Think of Hume's arguments against cause and effect. They are demolished, simply because nature is really there because God made it to be there, and being there the particulars of nature affect other particulars of nature which are there.

It is an intriguing thing (as we have already noted) that after the Reformation the Dutch painters began to paint nature. They no longer felt any necessity to restrict themselves always to religious subjects. As a matter of fact, after the Reformation religious subjects were relatively rarely painted. Most artists suddenly found that nature was worth painting, and that it is properly Christian to paint nature.

Now it follows that if we return to the Reformation, biblical view and nature is worth painting, so the nature which we paint is also worth something *in itself*. This is the true Christian mentality. It rests upon the reality of Creation-out-of-nothing by God. But it also follows that *all* things are equally created by God. *All* things were equally created out of nothing. *All* things, including man, are equal *in their origin*, as far as Creation is concerned.

All of this depends, of course, on the nature of God. Not only does God exist, but what kind of a God exists? The Judaistic-Christian God is completely different from all the other gods in the world. The Judaistic-Christian God is a Personal-Infinite God. The gods of the East are infinite by definition, in that they contain everything, including the male and female equally, the cruel and the non-cruel equally, and so on. But they are never personal. In contrast, the gods of the West, the Greek and the Roman gods, the great god Thor and the Anglo-Saxon gods, were personal but were always limited and finite.

So the Judaistic-Christian God is unique. He is Infinite, and He is Personal at the same time.

Now, how did He create? On the side of His infinity there is the the great chasm. He creates all things and He alone is Creator. Everything else is created. Only He is

Infinite and only He is the Creator; everything else is the creature and finite. Only He is independent; everything else is dependent. So man, the animal, the flower and the machine, in the biblical viewpoint, are equally separated from God, in that He created them all. On the side of infinity man is as separated from God as is the machine.

## THE PERSONAL-INFINITE GOD

|  |  |  |  |
|---|---|---|---|
|  |  |  | ========Chasm |
|  | Man | Man |  |
| Chasm== | ======= | Animal |  |
|  | Animal | Plant |  |
|  | Plant | Machine |  |
|  | Machine |  |  |

So on the side of the Infinite the chasm is between God and everything else, between the Creator and created things. But there is another side—the Personal. Here the animal, the flower and the machine are below the chasm. On the side of God's Infinity everything else is finite and equally separated from God; but on the side of His personality God has created man in His own image. Therefore man's relationship is upward rather than downward—a tremendous factor that opens door after door for the comprehension of confused modern man.

Man's relationship is not basically downward but upward. Man is separated, as personal, from nature because he is made in the image of God. That is, he has personality and as such he is unique in the creation, but he *is* united to all other creatures as being *created*. Man *is* separated from everything else, but that does not mean that there is not also a proper relationship downward on the side of man's being created and finite.

But his relationship is not *only* downward. Albert Schweitzer related himself to the hippopotamus coming through the bush, because Schweitzer had no sufficient relationship upward. This is wrong. Man is made in the image of God, who is personal, and has two relationships —upward and downward. Of course, if he does not find his relationship upward he will have to find his relationship (or integration point) downward. Christians reject this totally because we know who man is; we are not threatened by the machine as modern man is, because we know who we are. This is not said proudly, but humbly and reverently—we know we are made in the image of God. We reject an attitude that makes our integration point downward. Christians reject the view that there is no distinction—or only a quantitative distinction—between man and the other things; *and* they reject the view that man is totally separated from all the other things.

As a Christian I say, who am I? Am I only the hydrogen atom, the energy particle extended? No, I am made in the image of God. I know who I am. Yet, on the other hand, when I turn around and I face nature, I face something that is like myself. I, too, am created; just as the animal and the plant and the hydrogen atom are created.

There is a parallel here to our call to love. The Christian is told to love as brothers in Christ other Christians only. All men are not our brothers in Christ. The cry today in liberal theology is that everybody is a brother in Christ. From the biblical viewpoint brothers have the same father. Only when a man comes and casts himself upon the prophesied Messiah of the Old Testament as the Saviour, as he has come in His substitutionary work, does God become his Father. This is clear from the teaching of Jesus.

Therefore, not all men are our brothers in Christ. However, just because the Bible says that not all men are our brothers, it does not follow that we are not to love *all* men as our neighbours. So one has this tremendous impact of the teaching of Jesus about the Good Samaritan. Just because we are not commanded to love all men as our brothers in a special relationship does not negate for one second the call of God to love all men as our neighbours. In other words, I am to love on the basis of my neighbourliness all that which is one blood with myself. As a matter of fact, the New Testament uses that expression. 'One blood', to indicate the unity of all men by God's creation. We are people who know we have one common origin with all races, all languages and all people.

But only the Christian knows why he has a common origin. The evolutionist, the 'modern' man, has no real reason to understand a common origin or a common relationship among men, except a biological one: people breed—that is all they are left with.

The Christian, however, understands that we men are all from one origin. We are all of one flesh; we are of one blood. In other words, one can say that, from the biblical viewpoint, there are *two* humanities: the humanity on the one hand that stands in revolt against God and on the other hand the humanity that used to be in revolt against God (because none of us was at birth born into this second humanity). The members of this second group, having believed in Christ, have cast themselves upon God and have become the sons of God.

Yet one must never forget: there is only *one* humanity, and this is no paradox. There are orthodox Christians who will not let it be said that there is only one humanity, because they so strongly reject the liberal emphasis upon the one humanity at the expense of justification, but this is short-sighted. There are two humanities but there is one humanity: the Christian is called to understand that there are two humanities, and to love his brothers in Christ especially; and yet Christ also lays upon us the love of all men, as our neighbours, because we *are* one.

It is the same in regard to nature. On a very different level, we are separated from that which is the 'lower' form of creation, yet we are united to it. One must not

38

choose; one must say both. I am separated from it because I am made in the image of God: my integration point is upward, not downward; it is not turned back upon creation. Yet at the same time I am united to it by the fact that both nature and man are created by God.

This is a concept that no other philosophy has. Among other things, it explains the machine functions of man. For example, we have a common lung system with dogs and cats. This is not surprising. Both man and these other creatures have been created by God to fit a common environment. There is a common relationship in these mechanical functions, which relates man downward. There *are* machine functions to man. Psychologically there is a conditioning not only in the animals but also to some extent in man. This is to be expected, seeing that we have a relationship downward as well as a relationship upward. But nevertheless this is not my *basic* relationship. I am not afraid of the machine. I am not overwhelmed or threatened, because I know I am made in the image of God. I can see why I have mechanical functions and some conditioning, because I am related downward to the 'lower' things (though as we shall see the term 'lower' is not ideal). Therefore intellectually and psychologically, I look at these animals, plants and machines, and as I face them I understand something of the attitude I should have towards them. I begin to think differently about life. Nature begins to look different. I am separated from it, yet related to it.

Notice that phrase 'intellectually and psychologically'. This is a very important distinction. I can say, 'Yes, the tree is a creature as myself.' But that is not all that is involved. There ought to be a psychological insight too. Psychologically I ought to 'feel' a relationship to the tree as my fellow-creature. It is not simply that we ought to feel a relationship intellectually to the tree, and then turn this into just another argument for apologetics, but that we should realise, and train people in our churches to realise, that on the side of Creation and on the side of God's Infinity and our finiteness ... I really *am* one with the tree!

This relationship should not only be for aesthetic reasons—though that would be enough reason in itself, because beautiful things are important—but we should treat each thing with integrity because this is the way God has made it. So the Christian treats 'things' with integrity because we do not believe they are autonomous. Modern man has fallen into a dilemma because he has made things autonomous from God. Simone Weil's statement that modern man lives in a de-created world is acutely perceptive. Everything is de-created; everything is autonomous. But to Christians it is not autonomous, because God made it, and He made things on their own level. The value of the things is not in themselves autonomously, but that God made them, and thus they deserve to be treated with high respect. The tree in the field is to be treated with respect. It is not to be romanticised, like the old lady romanticising her cat (that is, she reads human reactions into it). This is wrong because it is not true. When you drive the axe into the tree, when you need firewood, you are not cutting down a person; you are cutting down a tree. So we do not romanticise the tree. But while we should not romanticise the tree, we must realise God made it and it deserves respect because He made it *as a tree*. Christians who do not believe in the complete evolutionary scale have reason to respect nature as the total evolutionist never can, because we believe God made these things specifically in their own areas. So if we are going to argue against the evolutionists intellectually, we should show the results of it in our attitudes. The Christian is a man who has a reason for dealing with each created thing on a high level of respect.

Now we warned earlier against allowing Platonic concepts to colour our Christian thinking. Platonism regards the material as low. But we certainly cannot think the material low when we realise that God made it. We can think of things being created in different order, but that is a very different concept from thinking things are 'low' in the sense of base, as opposed to 'high'. God made everything, and any sense of 'lowness' (with its other connotations) really has no place here. To think of them as low is really to insult the God who made them.

The second reason why the material is not low is because Christ's body was raised from the dead. This really is a very important point. The resurrection of the body should be held on to as a doctrinal reality, and not only a doctrinal reality but a truth that gives us an attitude towards life.

Christ's body really was raised from the dead. It could be touched and He could eat. And this resurrected body is now somewhere. We would reject Tillich's view of heaven as a 'philosophic other'. I think that John Robinson, in *Honest to God*, is right, from his viewpoint, in making the crucial point the ascension rather than the resurrection. I think he really understood the implications. A physical resurrection might happen somehow or other in the modern theologian's kind of a world, but what you could not have is a body that could eat, ascending into 'the philosophic other'. That is an unthinkable concept. So the ascension is very crucial. But we believe in the ascension, we believe the body of Jesus is somewhere in the unseen world. The resurrection and ascension prove there is no reason to make a false dichotomy between the spiritual and the material. That is a totally non-biblical concept. The material and the spiritual are not opposed. The fact that our bodies are going to be raised also speaks of this.

Another thing to notice from the biblical viewpoint is what I call God's convenant of creation. God has given us certain written covenants in the Scripture. He has made tremendous promises: for example, the covenant promise to Abraham and to the Jewish people; and the promise to the individual in the New Testament: 'He that believeth on the Son hath everlasting life.' God will not break his verbalised, propositional, written covenants in the Scripture.

But with God's written covenant there is also the convenant of creation (this is my own term). There are two kinds of covenant: a propositional, verbalised covenant in the Scriptures, and a covenant of creation, which rests upon the way God made things. God is going to deal with them *as He made them*. God will not violate either covenant. He will always deal with a plant as a plant, with an animal as an animal, with a machine as a machine and with a man as a man, not violating the orders of creation. He will not ask the machine to behave like a man, neither will He deal with man as though he is a machine.

So here is God treating His Creation with integrity: each thing in its own order, each thing the way He made it. If God treats His creation in that way, should we not treat our fellow-creature with a similar integrity? If God treats the tree like a tree, the machine like a machine and the man like a man, shouldn't I, as a fellow-creature, treat the machine like a machine, the man like a man, the plant like a plant—each thing in integrity in its own order? And for the highest reason: because I love God —I love the One who has made it! Loving the Lover who has made it, I should have respect for the thing He has made.

Now, let us emphasise, this is not pantheistic, but nevertheless this respect must be consciously exercised. *Consciously* we are to treat each thing in its own order and on its own level. Like so many things in the Christian life, this attitude does not come mechanically, because God is treating us like man and expects us to act like man. And in this situation we must *consciously* treat each thing in its own order and on its own level. We must deal with the integrity of each thing that we touch.

The good, modern architect has given a great deal of thought to a related thing, and in two ways. First of all, the good modern architect struggles to use materials with integrity. Consequently, for example, if he is using poured concrete, he wants it to look like poured concrete and not make it look like brick. The second area of integrity for the architect was emphasised by the great architect Wright, who put forward the concept of the integrity of the buildings to the integrity of the terrain. So there is this tremendous desire in our own day to treat material honestly. If we are to have something beautiful, a landscaping that's going to stand with strength, we shall have to keep in mind the integrity of the terrain and the integrity of the material used.

Now although this concept is true for all men, as they are made in the image of God even if they do not know it, yet Christians have a special understanding of it. God makes the thing well and He treats it with integrity. So I should treat it with integrity, not just for an aesthetic reason, but because this is the way God has made it and the way He deals with it. If He deals with the machine like a machine, and the man like a man, and the plant like a plant, and the animal like an animal, then we who say we are His creatures by choice and not just because we are creatures, surely now have a positive and dynamic and not just a static reason for our attitude: this is the way it ought to be. If I am going to be in the right relationship with God, I should treat the things He has made in the same way as He treats them.

So the value of the thing is not in itself autonomously! As I have emphasised in my previous books, as soon as we make anything autonomous we destroy everything. It is the same here: the value in nature is not in its value autonomously.

Now in sociological things modern man deals only with sociological 'averages'. But in the modern field of ecology he begins to scream, 'I am dying in my city and my ocean is dying.' This goes far beyond sociological 'averages'. His inner attitude to nature is involved. How is he treating it? Modern man has no real 'value' for the ocean. All he has is the most crass form of egoist, pragmatic value for it. He treats it as a 'thing' in the worst possible sense, to exploit for the 'good' of man. The man who believes things are only there by chance cannot give things a real value. But for the Christian the value of a thing is not in itself autonomously, but because God made it. It deserves this respect as something which was created by God, as man himself has been created by God.

Now it is true, as Lynn White points out, that much 'Christianity' is worse off in the area of ecology than animism. The animists think there are spirits in the trees and so they do not cut down the trees carelessly. So far as ecology is concerned, we must admit that he is right: much 'Christianity' has treated nature with less restraint than animism, not because Christianity does not have an answer but because we have not *acted on* the answer; not because Christianity does not have a view that gives a greater value to the tree than the animist can give it but because we haven't acted on the value that we know it has, or should know it has, as a creature of God.

This is an extension of Abraham Kuiper's sphere concept. He sees each of us as many men: the man in the state, the man who is the employer, the man who is the father, the elder in the church, the professor in the university ... each of these in a different sphere. But even though they are in different spheres at different times, yet a Christian is to act like a Christian *in each of the spheres*. The man is *always* there and *he is always a Christian under the norms of Scripture*, whether he is the man in the classroom or the man in the home.

Now here is the extension: I am a Christian, but not only a Christian. I am also the creature, the one who has been created; the one who is not autonomous dealing with these other things that equally are not autonomous; and as a Christian, I am *consciously* to deal with every other created thing with integrity, each thing in its proper sphere by creation.

So, to summarise this chapter, let us reiterate the fundamental fact—and that is, *God has made all men and all things*. He has made my body as well as my soul. He has made me as I am with the hungers of my body, as well as the hungers of my spirit. And He has made all things just as He has made me. He has made the stone, the star, the farthest reaches of the cosmos. He has done all this!

To think of any of these things as intrinsically low, is really an insult to the God who made it. Why did Christians lose their way, when it seems so clear and so definite? Why should I say my body is lower than my soul when God made both my body and my soul?

Secondly, Christ's incarnation teaches us that the body of man and nature is not to be considered as low. How can it be? After all, Jesus took on a real body because we—men— were made by God with a body.

So in the Incarnation the God of Creation took on a human body. But, more than that, after the resurrection Jesus Christ could eat and be touched. The Bible insists on the real, historic, space–time Resurrection of Jesus, so that there was a resurrected body that could eat and that could be touched. This body was not just a spirit—something to be viewed as an apparition or a 'ghost'—and this same body ascended into heaven, and went into the unseen world. And the body that can eat is still in the unseen world and will one day in future history be seen in the seen world again.

Our resurrection is of the same kind. When Christ comes back again our bodies are going to be raised from the dead. It is going to be a real physical resurrection, and consequently whether it is Jesus's body or our body the emphasis is the same: God has made the body and the body is not to be despised and considered as low.

The same sort of emphasis is found explicitly in God's covenant of Creation at the time of Noah. In Genesis 9:8–17 we have God's covenant within the relationship to Creation. 'And I, behold I established My covenant with you (mankind) and with your seed after you, and with every living created thing.' So God says this His covenant was with mankind, but equally with all creation. Then again, in the twelfth verse: 'This is the token of the covenant which I make between me and you and every living creature.' And in the thirteenth verse, He says: 'I set my bow in the cloud ... for a token of covenant between Me and the *earth*.' God makes a promise here that embodies *all* creation. God is interested in Creation. He does not despise it. There is no reason whatsoever, and it is indeed absolutely false biblically, for the Christian to have a Platonic view of nature. What God has made I, who am also a creature, must not despise.

## Chapter 5

## A Christian View: Substantial Healing

In Romans 8 Paul looks ahead to what is going to happen when Jesus Christ comes back again. He writes: 'For the earnest expectation of creation waiteth for the revealing of the sons of God (the Christians). For creation was made subject to vanity, not of its own will, but by reason of Him who has subjected it in hope. Because creation itself also shall be delivered from the bondage of corruption into the glorious liberty of the children of God. For we know that the whole creation groaneth and travaileth in pain together until now, and not only that, but ourselves also which had the first fruits of the Spirit (the Christians), even we ourselves groan within ourselves, waiting for the adoption, that is, the redemption of the body.'

What Paul says here is that when our bodies—bodies of men—are raised from the dead, at that time nature, too, will be redeemed. The blood of the Lamb will redeem man and nature together—as was the case in Egypt at the time of the Passover, when the blood applied to the doorposts saved not only the sons of the Hebrews but also their animals.

As we stressed in the last chapter, the Bible has no place at all for Platonic distinctions about nature. As Christ's death redeems men, including their bodies, from the consequences of the Fall, so His death will redeem all nature from its evil consequences, at the time when we are raised from the dead.

Now in Romans 6 Paul applies this future principle to our present situation. It is the great principle of Christian spirituality. Christ died, Christ is your Saviour, Christ is coming back again to raise you from the dead. So by faith, because this is true to what has been in Christ's death and to what will be when He comes again, by faith, in the power of the Holy Spirit, you are to live this way *substantially* now. 'Now if we be dead with Christ, we believe that we shall also live with Him ... Likewise reckon ye also yourselves to be dead indeed unto sin, but alive unto God through Jesus Christ our Lord.'

So we look forward to this, and one day it will be perfect. But we should be looking now, on the basis of the work of Christ, for substantial healing in every place affected by the Fall.

Now we must understand that even in our relationship with God a distinction has to be made here. By justification our guilt was completely removed, in a forensic way, as God declared our guilt gone when we accepted Christ as our Saviour. But, in practice, in our lives between becoming a Christian and the Second Coming of Christ or our death, we are not in a perfect relationship to God. Therefore real spirituality lies in the existential, moment by moment, looking to the blood of Christ, and upon the basis of the work of Christ seeking and asking God in faith for a substantial reality in our relationship with Him at the existential moment. I must be doing this so that substantially, in practice at this moment, there will be a reality in my relationship with the personal God who is there.

Now this is also true in other areas, because the Fall, as the Reformation theology has always emphasised, not only separated man from God but also caused other deep separations. It is interesting that almost the whole 'curse' in Genesis 3 is centred upon the outward manifestations. It is the *earth* that is going to be cursed for man's sake. It is the woman's *body* that is involved in the greatly multiplied conception and in pain in childbirth.

So there are other divisions. Man was divided from God, first; and then, ever since the Fall, man is separated from himself. These are the psychological divisions. I am convinced that this is the basic psychosis: that the individual man is divided from himself as a result of the Fall.

The next division is that man is divided from other men—and these are the sociological divisions. And then man is divided from nature and nature is divided from nature. So there are these multiple divisions, and one day when Christ comes back there is going to be a complete healing of all of them, on the basis of the 'blood of the Lamb'.

But Christians who believe the Bible are not simply called to say that 'one day' there will be healing, but that by God's grace substantially, upon the basis of the work of Christ, substantial healing can be a reality here and now.

Here the Church—the orthodox, Bible-believing Church—has been really poor. What have we done to heal sociological divisions? Often our churches are a scandal: they are cruel not only to the man 'outside' but also to the man 'inside'.

The same thing is true psychologically. We load people with psychological problems by telling them that 'Christians don't have breakdowns' ... and that is a kind of murder.

On the other hand, what we should have, individually and corporately, is a situation where, on the basis of the work of Christ, Christianity is seen to be not just 'pie in the sky', and where it is possible to have substantial healings now in every area where there are divisions because of the Fall. First of all my division from God is healed by justification, but then there must be the 'existential reality' moment by moment of this; secondly, there is the psychological division of man from himself; thirdly, the sociological divisions of man from other men; and lastly, the division of man from nature, and nature from nature. In all of these areas we should expect to see substantial healing.

I took a long while to settle on that word 'substantially', but it is, I think, the right word. It conveys the idea of a healing that is not *perfect*, but that is real, evident and substantial. Because of past history and future history, we are called upon to live this way by faith now.

When we carry these ideas over into the area of our relationship to nature, there is an exact parallel. On the basis of the fact that there is going to be total redemption in the future, not only of man but of all Creation, the Christian who believes the Bible should be the man who—with God's help and in the power of the Holy Spirit—is treating nature now in the direction of the way nature will be then. It will not now be perfect, but it must be substantial or we have missed our calling. God's calling to the Christian now—and to the Christian community—in the area of nature, just as it is in the area of personal Christian living in true spirituality, is that we should exhibit a substantial healing here and now, between man and nature and nature and itself, as far as Christians can bring it to pass.

Francis Bacon[1] wrote this: 'Man by the fall fell at the same time from his state of innocency and from his dominion over nature. Both of these losses, however, can even in this life be in some part repaired; the former by religion and faith, the latter by the arts and sciences.' It is a tragedy that the Church, including the orthodox, evangelical Church, has not always remembered that. Here, in this present life, it is possible for the Christian to have some share, through sciences and the arts, in returning nature to its proper place.

But how is this to be achieved? Firstly, as we have seen, by the emphasis upon Creation. Then, secondly, by a fresh understanding of man's 'dominion' over nature (Genesis 1 : 28). Man has dominion over the lower orders

[1] Bacon: *Novum Organon.*

of Creation, but he is not sovereign over them. Only God is the Sovereign Lord, and the lower orders are to be used with this truth in mind. Man is not using his own possessions.

A parallel is the gift of talents. They are to be used as God means them to be used. In the Parable of the Talents, told by Jesus (Matthew 25 : 14–30), the talents or money did not belong to the man with whom they were left. He was a servant and a steward, and he held them only in stewardship for the true owner.

When we have dominion over nature, *it is not ours*, either. It belongs to God, and we are to exercise our dominion over these things not as though entitled to exploit them, but as things borrowed or held in trust, which I am to use realising that they are not mine intrinsically. Man's dominion is under God's dominion and under God's domain.

Whenever anything is made autonomous, as I stressed in *Escape from Reason*, nature 'eats up' grace and soon all meaning is gone. And that is true here. When nature is made autonomous, either by the materialist, or by the Christian when he slips over and sits in the wrong place, soon *man eats up nature*. That is what we are seeing today. Suddenly man is beginning to scream, and I am convinced God is permitting these things to come to pass. The problem is not the population explosion alone —that could be handled. The problem, as White correctly points out, is the philosophy with which man has looked on nature.

An essential part of a true philosophy is a correct understanding of the pattern and plan of creation as revealed by the God who made it. For instance, we must see that each step 'higher'—the machine, the plant, the animal and man—has the use of that which is lower than itself. We find that man calls upon and utilises the animal, the plant and the machine; the animal eats the plant. The plant utilises the machine portion of the universe. Each thing, in God's creation, utilises the thing that God has made under it.

We must also appreciate that each thing is limited by what it is. That is, a plant is limited by being a plant, but it is also limited by the properties of those things under it that it uses. So the plants can only use the chemicals on the basis of the boundary condition of the chemicals' properties. There is nothing else it can do.

But this is true also for man. We cannot make our own universe; we can only use what is under us in the order of Creation. But there is a difference, and that is that the animal, for example, must use the lower *as what it is*. Man has to accept some necessary limitations of what is under him, but he can *consciously* act upon what is there. That is a real difference. The animal simply eats the plant. He cannot change its situation or properties. The man, on the other hand, has to accept some limitations, but nevertheless is called upon in his relationship to nature to treat the thing that is under him *consciously*, on the basis of what God has made it to be. The animal, the plant *must* do it; the man *should* do it. We are to use it, but we are not to use it as though it were nothing in itself.

Now let us look at it in another way. Man was given dominion over Creation. This is true. But since the Fall man has exercised this dominion wrongly. He is a rebel who has set himself at the centre of the universe. By Creation man has dominion; but as a fallen creature he has used that dominion wrongly. Because he is fallen, he exploits created things as though they were nothing in themselves, and as though he has an autonomous right to them.

Surely, then, Christians, who have returned through the work of the Lord Jesus Christ to fellowship with God, and have a proper place of reference to the God who is there, should demonstrate a proper use of nature. We are to have dominion over it, but we are not going to use it as fallen man uses it. We are not going to act as though it were nothing in itself, or as though we will do to nature everything we can do.

A parallel is man's dominion over woman. At the Fall —not before it, I think, but at it—man was given dominion in the home over the woman. But fallen man takes this and he turns it into tyranny and makes his wife a slave. So, first in the judaistic teaching, the Old Testament law, and then later and more specifically in the New Testament, man is taught to exercise dominion without tyranny. The man is to be the head of the home, but the man is also to love his wife as Christ loves the Church. Thus everything is back in its right place. There is to be order in the midst of a fallen world, but in love.

So man has dominion over nature, but he uses it wrongly. The Christian is called upon to exhibit this dominion, but exhibit it rightly: treating the thing as having value in itself, exercising dominion without being destructive. The Church should always have taught and done this, but she has generally failed to do so, and we need to confess our failure. Francis Bacon understood this, and so have other Christians at different times, but by and large we must say that for a long, long time Christian teachers, including the best, orthodox theologians, have shown a real poverty here.

As a parallel example, what would have happened, for example, if the Church at the time of the Industrial Revolution had spoken out against the economic abuses which arose from it? This is not to suggest that the Industrial Revolution was wrong, or that capitalism as such is necessarily wrong, but that the Church, at a point in history when it had the consensus, as it does not have now, failed (with some notable exceptions) to speak against the abuse of economic dominion. So also the Church has not spoken out as it should have done throughout history against the abuse of nature.

But when the Church puts belief into practice, in man

*and in nature*, there is substantial healing. And one of the first fruits of that healing is a new sense of beauty. The aesthetic values are not to be despised. God has made man with a sense of beauty, in a way no animal has: no animal has ever produced a work of art. Man as made in the image of God has an aesthetic quality, and as soon as he begins to deal with nature as he should—as having dominion but not exploiting nature as though it had no value in itself, and realising it is also a creature of God as man is, beauty is preserved in nature. But also, economic and human value will accrue, for the problems of ecology that we have now will diminish.

Christians should be able to exhibit individually and corporately that—on the basis of the work of Christ, dealing with things according to the world view and basic philosophy of the Bible—they can produce something that the world has tried to produce and failed. The Christian community should be a living exhibition of the truth that in our present situation it is possible to have substantial sociological healings—healings that humanism longs for but has not been able to produce. Humanism is not wrong in its cry for sociological healing, but humanism is not producing it. And the same thing is true in regard to a substantial healing where nature is concerned.

So we find that when we begin to deal on a Christian basis, things begin to change; not just theoretical things, important as they are, but practical things. Man is not to be sacrificed, as pantheism sacrifices him, because, after all, he was made in the image of God, and given dominion. And yet nature is to be honoured, each thing on its own level. In other words, there is a balance here. Man has dominion; he has a right by choice, because he is also by choice a moral creature—a right by choice to have dominion. But he is to exercise it rightly. He is to honour what God has made up to the very highest level that he can honour it, without sacrificing man.

Christians, of all people, should not be the destroyers. We should treat nature with an overwhelming respect. We may cut down a tree to build a house, or to make a fire to keep the family warm. But we should not cut down the tree just to cut down the tree. We may, if necessary, bark the cork tree in order to have the use of the bark. But what we may not do is to bark the tree simply for the sake of doing so, and let it dry and stand there a dead skeleton in the wind. To so do is not to treat the tree with integrity. We have the right to rid our houses of ants; but what we have no right to do is to forget to honour the ant as God made it, out in the place where God made the ant to be. When we meet the ant on the pavement, we step over him. He is a creature, like ourselves; not made in the image of God, it is true, but equal with man as far as Creation is concerned. The ant and the man are both creatures.

In this sense St. Francis's use of the term 'brothers' to the birds is not only theologically correct but a thing to be intellectually thought of and practically practised. More, it is to be psychologically felt as I face the tree, the bird, the ant. If this was what The Doors had meant when they spoke of 'Our Fair Sister', it would be beautiful. Why have orthodox evangelical Christians produced no hymns putting such a beautiful concept in a proper theological setting?

One does not deface things simply to deface them. One would not willingly deface the rock. After all, the rock has a God-given right to be the rock. If you must move the rock in order to build the foundation of a house—then, by all means, move it. But do not strip the moss from it and leave it to lie by the side and die. Even the moss has a right to live. It is equal with man as a creature of God.

Hunting game is another example of the same principle. The killing of animals for food is one thing, but on the other hand they do not exist simply as things to be

55

slaughtered. This is true of fishing, too. Many men fish and leave their victims to rot and stink. But what about the fish? Has he no rights—not to be romanticised as though he was a man, but real rights? On the one hand it is wrong to treat the fish as though it were a human baby; yet, on the other hand, neither is it merely a chip of wood.

When we consider the tree, which is 'below' the fish, we may chop it down, so long as we remember it is a tree, with its own value *as a tree*. It is not a zero. Some of our housing demonstrates the practical application of this. Bulldozers have gone in to flatten everything and clear the trees before the houses are begun. The end result is ugliness. It would have cost another thousand pounds to bulldoze *round* the trees, so they are simply bulldozed down without question. And then we wonder, looking at the result, how people can live there. It is less human in its barrenness, and even economically it is poorer as the top-soil washes away. So when man breaks God's truth, in reality he suffers.

The hippies are right in their desire to be close to nature, even walking in bare feet in order to feel it. But they have no philosophy, and so it drifts into pantheism, and soon becomes ugly. But Christians, who should understand the creation principle, have a reason for respecting nature, and when they do, it results in benefits to man. Let us be clear it is not just a pragmatic attitude; there is a basis for it. We treat it with respect because God made it. When an orthodox evangelical Christian mistreats or is insensible to nature, *at that point* he is more wrong than the hippie who has no real basis for his feeling for nature and yet senses that man and nature should have a relationship beyond that of spoiler and spoiled. You may, or may not, want to walk bare-foot to feel close to nature, but *as a Christian* what relationship have you thought of and practised towards nature as your fellow-creature, over the last ten years?

Why do I have an emotional reaction towards the tree? For some abstract or pragmatic reason? Not at all. Secular man may say he cares for the tree because if he cuts it down his cities will not be able to breathe. But that is egoism, and egoism will produce ugliness, no matter how long it takes. On this basis technology will take another twist on the garrote of both nature and man. The tyranny of technology will grow to be almost totally complete. But the Christian stands in front of the tree, and has an emotional reaction towards it, because the tree has a real value in itself, being a creature made by God, just as my value is that I am made by God and not just cast up by chance. The tree, too, has been made by God, and it was not cast up by chance, either.

Suddenly, then, we have real beauty. Life begins to breathe. The world begins to breathe as it never breathed before. We can love a man for his own sake, for we know who the man is—he is made in the image of God; and we can care for the animal, the tree and even the machine portion of the universe, each thing in its own order—for we know what it is as a fellow-creature with ourselves, both made by the same God.

# Chapter 6

## The Christian View: The 'Pilot Plant'

So we have seen that a truly biblical Christianity has a real answer to the ecological crisis. It offers a balanced and healthy attitude to nature, arising from the truth of its creation by God; it offers the hope here and now of substantial healing in nature of some of the results of the Fall, arising from the truth of redemption in Christ. In each of the alienations arising from the Fall the Christians, individually and corporately, should consciously in practice be a redemptive factor. By God's Grace they should consciously in practice be a healing, redemptive factor in this life in the separation of man from God, man from himself, man from man, man from nature and nature from nature. And certainly this is true in regard to nature. A Christian-based science and technology should consciously try to see nature substantially healed, while waiting for the coming complete healing at Christ's return.

Now in this final chapter, we must ask how the Christian Church, believing these truths, can apply them practically to the whole question of ecology.[1]

For here is our calling. We must exhibit that, on the basis of the work of Christ, the Church can achieve partially, but substantially, what the secular world wants and cannot get. The Church—to put it another way—ought to be a 'pilot plant', where men can see in our congregations and missions a substantial healing of all

[1] My wife's book, *Hidden Art* by Edith Schaeffer (The Norfolk Press, 1970), includes many practical areas in regard to the proper use of nature.

the divisions, the alienations, man's rebellion has produced.

Let me explain that phrase 'pilot plant'. When an industrial company is about to construct a big plant, it first of all makes a 'pilot' plant. This is to demonstrate that the full-scale plant can work. Now the Church, I believe, ought to be a 'pilot plant' concerning the healing of man and himself, of man and man, and man and nature. Indeed, unless something like this happens, I do not believe the world will listen to what we have to say. For instance, in the area of nature, we ought to be exhibiting the very opposite of the situation I described earlier, where the pagans who had their wine stomps provided a beautiful setting for the Christians to look at, while the Christians provided something ugly for the pagans to see! That sort of situation must be reversed, or our words and our philosophy will—not surprisingly—be ignored.

So the Christian Church ought to be this 'pilot plant', through individual attitudes and the Christian community's attitude, to exhibit that in this present life men can exercise dominion over nature without being destructive. Let me give two illustrations of what this might involve. The first is open-face or strip-mining.

Why does strip-mining turn the world into an absolute desert? Why is the 'Black Country' in England's Midlands 'black'? What has brought about this ugly destruction of the environment? There is only one reason: man's greed.

If the strip-miners would take bulldozers and push back the top-soil, then rip out the coal, put back the soil and push back the top-soil, then ten years after the coal was removed there would be a green field, and in fifty years a forest. But, as it stands, for an added profit above what is reasonable in regard to nature, man turns these areas into deserts—and then pretty soon cries out that the top-soil is gone, that grass will not grow, and there is no way for hundreds of years to grow trees!

It is always true that if you treat the land properly, you have to make two choices. The first is in the area of economics. It costs more money, at least at first, to treat the land well. For instance, in the case of the school I have mentioned, all they had to do to improve the place was plant trees to shield the building they had put up. But it costs money to plant trees, and somebody decided that instead of planting trees they would prefer to do something else with the money. Of course, the school needs money for its important work: but there is a time when planting trees *is* an important work.

The second choice involved is that it usually takes longer to treat the land properly. And these are the two factors that lead to the destruction of our environment: money and time—or, to say it another way, greed and haste. The question is, or seems to be, are we going to have an immediate profit, and an immediate saving of time; or are we going to do what we really should do as God's children?

Apply this to strip-mining. There is no reason in the world why strip-mining was compelled to leave western Pennsylvania like it is. Strip-mines, as we have seen, do not have to be left this way: the soil can be bulldozed back. What we, the Christian community, have to do is to refuse men the right to ravish our land, just as we refuse them the right to ravish our women; to insist that somebody accepts a little less profit by not exploiting nature. And the first step is exhibiting the fact that as individual Christians and as Christian communities, we ourselves do not ravish our 'fair sister' for the sake of greed, in one form or another.

We can see the same sort of thing happening in Switzerland. Here is a village up in the mountains somewhere. It has never had electricity. It has got along for a thousand years, in fact, without electricity. Now, suddenly, civilisation comes, and everybody knows that you cannot have civilisation without electricity, so the decision is taken to give the village electrical power.

Now this can be done in one of two ways. They can have their electricity in about three months: just chop off everything, tear the forest in pieces, run big, heavy wires over the whole thing, and create ugliness out of what was beautiful. Or they can wait a couple of years for their electricity: then we can handle the cables and the forests with more care, hiding what we need to hide and considering the integrity of the environment, and end up with something infinitely preferable—they have their electricity *and* the village has its beauty . . . and the only cost is to add two years to the thousand years that they have been without electricity. There would be some economic factors here, but the largest one is that of sheer haste.

Or think of the highways—our asphalt jungle. Think, if you will, of the way we use our bulldozers across the Swiss mountains. *Almost always* the scars and the ugliness are results of hurry. And whether it is hurry or greed, these things eat away at nature.

But as Christians we have to learn to say 'Stop'. Because, after all, greed is destructive at this point against nature, and there is a time to take one's time.

Now all this will not come about automatically. Science today treats man as less than man, and nature as less than nature. And the reason for this is that modern science has the wrong sense of *origin*, and having the wrong sense of origin it has no category sufficient to treat nature as nature any more than it has to treat man as man.

Nevertheless, we, who are Christians, must be careful. We must confess that we missed our opportunity. We have spoken loudly against materialistic science, but we have done little to show that in practice we ourselves as Christians are not dominated by a technological orientation in regard either to man or nature. We should have been stressing and practising for a long time that there is a basic reason why we should not do all we can do. But have we missed the opportunity to help man save his earth. Not only that, but in our generation we are losing an evangelistic opportunity, because when modern young people—many of them—have a real sensitivity to nature, they turn to the hippy communities or mentality, where there is at least a genuine sense of nature (even if a wrong one), because they have seen that most Christians simply do not care about the beauty of nature, or nature as such.

So we have not only missed our opportunity to save the earth for man but this also partly accounts for the fact that we have largely missed an opportunity of reaching the twentieth century. These are reasons why the Church seems irrelevant and helpless in our generation. We are living in and practising a sub-Christianity.

There is a parallel between man's misuse of nature and man's misuse of man. We can see this in two areas.

First of all, let us think of the sex relationship. What is man's attitude towards the girl? It is possible, and common in the modern setting, to have a 'playboy' attitude; or, rather, a 'plaything' attitude, where 'the playmate becomes the plaything'. Here, the girl is no more than a sex object.

But what is the Christian view? Somebody may put forward at this point the rather romantic notion, 'You shouldn't look for any pleasure for yourself, you should just look for the other person's pleasure'. But that is not what the Bible says. We are not to love our neighbour *as ourselves*. We have a right to pleasure, too. But what we do not have a right to do is to forget that the girl is a person and not an animal, a plant or a machine. We have the right to have our pleasure in a sexual relationship, but we have no right whatsoever to exploit a partner as a sex object.

There should be a conscious limitation upon our pleasure. We impose a limit—a *self-imposed* limit—in order to treat the girl fairly as a person. So, although a man *could* do more, he does not do everything he could do, because he must treat her also as a person and not just as a thing with no value. And if he does so treat her, eventually he loses, because love is gone, and all that is left is just a mechanical, chemical sexuality and humanity is lost as he treats her as less than human. Eventually, not only her humanity is diminished, but his is. In contrast, if he does less than he could do, eventually he has more, for he has a human relationship, he has love and not just a chemical act. It is like the principle of the boomerang—it goes full circle and destroys the destroyer. *And that is exactly what happens with nature.* If we treat nature as having no intrinsic value, our own value is diminished.

A second parallel may be found with man in business. We have all kinds of idealists today who cry, 'No profit! Down with the profit motive!' But men do not work this way. Even Communism is learning the need to reinstate the profit motive. And certainly the Bible does not say that the profit motive is wrong as such.

But I am to treat the man I deal with in business *as myself*. I am to 'love' him as my neighbour, and as myself. It is perfectly right that I should have some profit, but I must not get it by treating him (or exploiting him) as a consumer object. If I do this—treat the man merely as a consumer object—eventually I shall destroy not him only, but myself, because I shall have lowered the real value of myself.

So, just as the girl is not to be treated as a sex object but as a person, so again I must, if I am a businessman, functioning on a Christian basis, realise I am dealing with another man made in the image of God, and I must impose some conscious limitation on myself. The Christian businessman will take profit, but he will not do everything he could do in exacting all the profit he could exact.

The Old Testament is very plain at this point: If you take a man's cloak for a collateral, be sure to give it back to him every night, because he might be cold at night ...[2] Again: 'No man shall take the nether or the upper millstone to pledge: for he takes a man's *life* to pledge.'[3] That shows a very different mentality from that which often marks Christian businessmen. It may properly be called capitalism, but it is a very different kind of capitalism. It realises that if we treat other men in business or in industry as machines, we make ourselves machines, because we are not more than they are. Indeed, if we make other men and ourselves machines in commercial relationships, gradually this will penetrate every area of life and the wonder of humanity will begin to disappear.

Thus again the Christian does not do all he can do. He has a limiting principle, and in doing less he has more, for his own 'humanness' is at stake. A girl should not be treated as a sex object to be used simply for pleasure. A man should not be treated as a consumer object simply for bigger profit. In the area of sex, and in the area of business eventually, too, to treat persons as they should be treated, on the basis of the Creation of God, is not only right in itself but produces good results, because our humanity begins to bloom.

In the area of nature it is exactly the same. If nature is only a meaningless particular, is 'de-created'—to use Simone Weil's evocative word—only a meaningless particular in a de-created world, with no universal to give it any meaning—then wonder is gone from it. Unless there is a universal over the particulars, there is no meaning.

Jean-Paul Sartre picks this up: if you have a finite point and it has no infinite reference point, then that finite point is absurd. And he is right; and, unhappily, that is where he himself is—an absurd particular in the midst of only absurd particulars.

[2] See Exodus 22:26.

[3] Deuteronomy 24:6.

So, if nature and the things of nature are only a meaningless series of particulars in a de-created universe, with no universal to give them meaning, then nature is become absurd, wonder is gone from it ... and wonder is equally gone from me, because I too am a finite thing. If the wonder is gone from nature, then the wonder will gradually go from me because I too am finite.

But Christians insist that we do have a universal. God is there! The personal-infinite God is the universal of all the particulars, because He created all the particulars and in his verbalised, propositional communication in the Scriptures He has given us categories within which to treat everything within His creation: man to man, man to nature, the whole lot.

Thus, as I look at things on this basis, as a Christian, I am not without a universal to give meaning to nature and meaning to man. I am aware of a marvellous universal: a personal God, who has created the world, who has a character and who has given His verbalised, propositional communication in a true revelation. Now both the thing that He has made and I, who am also made by Him, have wonder, awe and real value.

But we must remember that the value I consciously put on a thing—each on its own level—will finally be my own value, for I too am finite. If I let the wonder go from the thing, soon the wonder will go from mankind and from me. And this is where we live today. The wonder is all gone. Man sits in his autonomous 'de-created' world, where there are no universals and no wonder in nature. Indeed, in an arrogant and egoistic way, nature has been reduced to a 'thing' for man to use or exploit. And if modern man speaks of protecting the ecological balance of nature, it is only on the pragmatic level for man, with no basis for nature having any real value in itself. And thus man, too, is reduced another notch in value and dehumanised technology takes another turn on the vice.

On the other hand, in the Christian view of things nature is restored. Suddenly, the wonder returns.

But it is not enough merely to believe that there is a real meaning in nature, as a matter of theory. The truth has to be practised consciously. We have to begin to treat nature the way it *should* be treated.

We have seen in regard to the pleasure of sex, and in the making of profit in industry and business, that man must put a *self* limitation on himself. He must not be driven either for greed, or haste, to remove all the self limitations. Or we can put it in another way: that we must not allow ourselves, individually, nor our technology, to do everything we or it can do.

Now if we are going to put a true understanding of nature into practice it will mean a limitation. The animal can make no conscious limitation. The cow eats the grass —it has no decision to make. It cannot do otherwise. Its only limitation is the limitation of its 'cowness'. I who am made in the image of God can make a choice. I am able to do things to nature that I should not do. So I am to put a *self* limitation on what is possible. The horror and ugliness of modern man in his technology and in his individual life is that he does everything he can do, without limitation. Everything he *can* do he *does*. He kills the world, he kills mankind and he kills himself.

There are two kinds of limitations: of the cow—a mechanical limitation; and the limitation of man, which has mechanical limitations but also limitations which are voluntary and conscious.

I am a being made in the image of God. Having a rational-moral limitation, not everything man can do is right to do. Indeed, this is the problem all the way back to the Garden of Eden. From the point of view of body structure, Eve could eat the fruit; Adam could eat the fruit. But on the basis of the second boundary condition of the moral command of God, and the character of God, it was wrong for them to eat the fruit. The call was for

Eve to limit herself: to refrain from doing something she could do.

Technologically, modern man does everything he can do—he functions on this single boundary principle. Modern man, seeing himself as autonomous, with no personal-infinite God who has spoken, has no adequate universal to supply an adequate second boundary condition; and man being fallen is not only finite but sinful. Thus man's pragmatically made choices have no reference point beyond human egotism. It is dog eat dog, man eat man, man eat nature. Man with his greed has no real reason not to rape nature, and treat it as a reverse 'consumer object'. Nature as such is without value or rights.

In conclusion, then, we may say that if things are treated only as autonomous machines in a de-created world they are finally meaningless. But if that is so, then inevitably so am I—man—autonomous and also equally meaningless. But if individually and in the Christian community I treat with integrity the things which God had made, and treat them this way lovingly, because they are His, things *change*. If I love the Lover, I love what the Lover has made. Perhaps this is the reason why so many Christians feel an unreality in their Christian lives. If I don't love what the Lover has made—in the area of man, in the area of nature—and really love it *because He made it*—do I really love the Lover at all?

It is easy to make professions of faith, but they may not be worth much because they have no real meaning. They may become merely a mental assent that means nothing, or much too little in a much too limited area, in reality.

But I must be clear that I am not loving the tree or whatever is standing in front of me, for a pragmatic reason. It will have a pragmatic *result*, the very pragmatic results that the men involved in ecology are looking for. But as a Christian I do not do it for the practical or pragmatic results; I do it because it is right and because God is the Maker; and then suddenly things drop into place.

There are things before me which I now face, not as a cow would face the buttercup—merely the mechanical situation—but facing it by choice. I look at the buttercup, and I treat the buttercup the way it should be treated. The buttercup and I are both created by God, but beyond this, I can treat it properly by personal choice. I act personally—and I am a person! Psychologically I begin to breathe and live. Psychologically I am now dealing on a personal level, not only with men and women but also with the things in nature that God has made which are less than personal in themselves—and the old hang-ups begin to crumble. My humanness grows and the modern technological pit and pendulum is no longer closing in on me.

And then, secondly, suddenly there is beauty instead of a desert. The question of aesthetics is also in place. This surely is something that has importance in itself. Beauty is not to be despised as a thing in itself. It does not have to have pragmatic reasons to have value. So if we did nothing else in our Christian view of nature than save and enjoy beauty, it would be of value, and worth while.

But it is not only that, as we have seen. The balance of nature will be more what it should be, and there will be a way to utilise nature for man and yet not destroy the resources which man needs. But none of this will happen if it is only a gimmick. And we have to be in the right relationship with Him in the way He has provided, and then, as Christians, have and practise the Christian view of nature.

When we have learnt this—the Christian view of nature—then there can be a real ecology; beauty will flow; psychological freedom will come, and the world will cease being turned into a desert. Because it is right, on the basis of the whole Christian system—which is strong enough to stand it all, because it is true—as I stand, as a creature, and face the buttercup, I say, 'Fellow-creature, fellow-*creature*, I won't walk on you. We are both creatures together.'

# Appendix I

## The Historical Roots of Our Ecologic Crisis
### *Lynn White, Jr.*[1]

A conversation with Aldous Huxley not infrequently put one at the receiving end of an unforgettable monologue. About a year before his lamented death he was discoursing on a favourite topic: Man's unnatural treatment of nature and its sad results. To illustrate his point he told how, during the previous summer, he had returned to a little valley in England where he had spent many happy months as a child. Once it had been composed of delightful grassy glades; now it was becoming overgrown with unsightly brush because the rabbits that formerly kept such growth under control had largely succumbed to a disease, myxomatosis, that was deliberately introduced by the local farmers to reduce the rabbits' destruction of crops. Being something of a Philistine, I could be silent no longer, even in the interests of great rhetoric. I interrupted to point out that the rabbit itself had been brought as a domestic animal to England in 1176, presumably to improve the protein diet of the peasantry.

All forms of life modify their contexts. The most spectacular and benign instance is doubtless the coral polyp. By serving its own ends, it has created a vast undersea world favourable to thousands of other kinds of animals and plants. Ever since man became a numerous species he has affected his environment notably. The hypothesis that his fire-drive method of hunting created

[1] The author is professor of history at the University of California, Los Angeles. This is the text of a lecture delivered December 26, 1966, at the Washington meeting of the A.A.A.S.

the world's great grasslands and helped to exterminate the monster mammals of the Pleistocene from much of the globe is plausible, if not proved. For six millenia at least, the banks of the lower Nile have been a human artifact rather than the swampy African jungle which nature, apart from man, would have made it. The Aswan Dam, flooding 5,000 square miles, is only the latest stage in a long process. In many regions terracing or irrigation, overgrazing, the cutting of forests by Romans to build ships to fight Carthaginians or by Crusaders to solve the logistics problems of their expeditions, have profoundly changed some ecologies. Observation that the French landscape falls into two basic types, the open fields of the north and the *bocage* of the south and west, inspired Marc Bloch to undertake his classic study of medieval agricultural methods. Quite unintentionally, changes in human ways often affect non-human nature. It has been noted, for example, that the advent of the automobile eliminated huge flocks of sparrows that once fed on the horse manure littering every street.

The history of ecologic change is still so rudimentary that we know little about what really happened, or what the results were. The extinction of the European aurochs as late as 1627 would seem to have been a simple case of over-enthusiastic hunting. On more intricate matters it often is impossible to find solid information. For a thousand years or more the Frisians and Hollanders have been pushing back the North Sea, and the process is culminating in our own time in the reclamation of the Zuider Zee. What, if any, species of animals, birds, fish, shore life or plants have died out in the process? In their epic combat with Neptune have the Netherlanders overlooked ecological values in such a way that the quality of human life in the Netherlands has suffered? I cannot discover that the questions have ever been asked, much less answered.

People, then, have often been a dynamic element in

71

their own environment, but in the present state of historical scholarship we usually do not know exactly when, where, or with what effects man-induced changes came. As we enter the last third of the twentieth century, however, concern for the problem of ecologic backlash is mounting feverishly. Natural science, conceived as the effort to understand the nature of things, has flourished in several eras and among several peoples. Similarly there had been an age-old accumulation of technological skills, sometimes growing rapidly, sometimes slowly. But it was not until about four generations ago that Western Europe and North America arranged a marriage between science and technology, a union of the theoretical and the empirical approaches to our natural environment. The emergence in widespread practice of the Baconian creed that scientific knowledge means technological power over nature can scarcely be dated before about 1850, save in the chemical industries, where it is anticipated in the eighteenth century. Its acceptance as a normal pattern of action may mark the greatest event in human history since the invention of agriculture, and perhaps in non-human terrestrial history as well.

Almost at once the new situation forced the crystallisation of the novel concept of ecology; indeed, the word *ecology* first appeared in the English language in 1873. Today, less than a century later, the impact of our race upon the environment has so increased in force that it has changed in essence. When the first cannons were fired, in the early fourteenth century, they affected ecology by sending workers scrambling to the forests and mountains for more potash, sulphur, iron ore and charcoal, with some resulting erosion and deforestation. Hydrogen bombs are of a different order: a war fought with them might alter the genetics of all life on this planet. By 1285 London had a smog problem arising from the burning of soft coal, but our present combustion of fossil fuels threatens to change the chemistry of the globe's atmosphere as a whole, with consequences which we are only beginning to guess. With the population explosion, the carcinoma of planless urbanism, the now geological deposits of sewage and garbage, surely no creature other than man has ever managed to foul its nest in such short order.

There are many calls to action, but specific proposals, however worthy as individual items, seem too partial, palliative, negative: ban the bomb, tear down the billboards, give the Hindus contraceptives and tell them to eat their sacred cows. The simplest solution to any suspect change is, of course, to stop it, or, better yet, to revert to a romanticised past: make those ugly petrol stations look like Anne Hathaway's cottage or (in the Far West) like ghost-town saloons. The 'wilderness area' mentality invariably advocates deep-freezing an ecology, whether San Gimigano or the High Sierra, as it was before the first Kleenex was dropped. But neither atavism nor prettification will cope with the ecologic crisis of our time.

What shall we do? No one yet knows. Unless we think about fundamentals, our specific measures may produce new backlashes more serious than those they are designed to remedy.

As a beginning we should try to clarify our thinking by looking, in some historical depth, at the presuppositions that underlie modern technology and science. Science was traditionally aristocratic, speculative, intellectual in intent; technology was lower-class, empirical, action-oriented. The quite sudden fusion of these two, towards the middle of the nineteenth century, is surely related to the slightly prior and contemporary democratic revolutions which, by reducing social barriers, tended to assert a functional unity of brain and hand. Our ecologic crisis is the product of an emerging, entirely novel, democratic culture. The issue is whether a democratised world can survive its own implications. Presumably we cannot unless we rethink our axioms.

## The Western Traditions of Technology and Science

One thing is so certain that it seems stupid to verbalise it : both modern technology and modern science are distinctively *Occidental*. Our technology has absorbed elements from all over the world, notably from China; yet everywhere today, whether in Japan or in Nigeria, successful technology is Western. Our science is the heir to all the sciences of the past, especially perhaps to the work of the great Islamic scientists of the Middle Ages, who so often outdid the ancient Greeks in skill and perspicacity : al-Rāzī in medicine, for example; or ibn-al-Haytham in optics; or Omar Khayyám in mathematics. Indeed, not a few works of such geniuses seem to have vanished in the original Arabic and to survive only in medieval Latin translations that helped to lay the foundations for later Western developments. Today, around the globe, all significant science is Western in style and method, whatever the pigmentation or language of the scientists.

A second pair of facts is less well recognised because they result from quite recent historical scholarship. The leadership of the West, both in technology and in science, is far older than the so-called Scientific Revolution of the seventeenth century or the so-called Industrial Revolution of the eighteenth century. These terms are in fact outmoded and obscure the true nature of what they try to describe—significant stages in two long and separate developments. By A.D. 1000 at the latest—and perhaps, feebly, as much as two hundred years earlier—the West began to apply water power to industrial processes other than milling grain. This was followed in the late twelfth century by the harnessing of wind power. From simple beginnings, but with remarkable consistency of style, the West rapidly expanded its skills in the develop-

74

ment of power machinery, labour-saving devices and automation. Those who doubt should contemplate that most monumental achievement in the history of automation: the weight-driven mechanical clock, which appeared in two forms in the early fourteenth century. Not in craftsmanship but in basic technological capacity, the Latin West of the later Middle Ages far outstripped its elaborate, sophisticated and aesthetically magnificent sister cultures, Byzantium and Islam. In 1444 a great Greek ecclesiastic, Bessarion, who had gone to Italy, wrote a letter to a prince in Greece. He is amazed by the superiority of Western ships, arms, textiles, glass. But above all he is astonished by the spectacle of water-wheels sawing timbers and pumping the bellows of blast furnaces. Clearly, he had seen nothing of the sort in the Near East.

By the end of the fifteenth century the technological superiority of Europe was such that its small, mutually hostile nations could spill out over all the rest of the world, conquering, looting and colonising. The symbol of this technological superiority is the fact that Portugal, one of the weakest states of the Occident, was able to become, and to remain for a century, mistress of the East Indies. And we must remember that the technology of Vasco da Gama and Albuquerque was built by pure empiricism, drawing remarkably little support or inspiration from science.

In the present-day vernacular understanding, modern science is supposed to have begun in 1543, when both Copernicus and Vesalius published their great works. It is no derogation of their accomplishments, however, to point out that such structures as the *Fabrica* and the *De revolutionibus* do not appear overnight. The distinctive Western tradition of science, in fact, began in the late eleventh century with a massive movement of translation of Arabic and Greek scientific works into Latin. A few notable books—Theophrastus, for example—escaped the

West's avid new appetite for science, but within less than two hundred years effectively the entire corpus of Greek and Muslim science was available in Latin, and was being eagerly read and criticised in the new European universities. Out of criticism arose new observation, speculation and increasing distrust of ancient authorities. By the late thirteenth century Europe had seized global scientific leadership from the faltering hands of Islam. It would be as absurd to deny the profound originality of Newton, Galileo or Copernicus as to deny that of the fourteenth-century scholastic scientists like Buridan or Oresme on whose work they built. Before the eleventh century, science scarcely existed in the Latin West, even in Roman times. From the eleventh century onward, the scientific sector of Occidental culture has increased in a steady crescendo.

Since both our technological and our scientific movements got their start, acquired their character and achieved world dominance in the Middle Ages, it would seem that we cannot understand their nature or their present impact upon ecology without examining fundamental medieval assumptions and developments.

## Medieval View of Man and Nature

Until recently, agriculture has been the chief occupation even in 'advanced' societies; hence, any change in methods of tillage has much importance. Early ploughs, drawn by two oxen, did not normally turn the sod but merely scratched it. Thus, cross-ploughing was needed and fields tended to be squarish. In the fairly light soils and semi-arid climates of the Near East and Mediterranean, this worked well. But such a plough was inappropriate to the wet climate and often sticky soils of northern Europe. By the latter part of the seventh century after Christ, however, following obscure beginnings, certain northern peasants were using an entirely new

76

kind of plough, equipped with a vertical knife to cut the line of the furrow, a horizontal share to slice under the sod and a mouldboard to turn it over. The friction of this plough with the soil was so great that it normally required not two but eight oxen. It attacked the land with such violence that cross-ploughing was not needed, and fields tended to be shaped in long strips.

In the days of the scratch-plough, fields were distributed generally in units capable of supporting a single family. Subsistence farming was the presupposition. But no peasant owned eight oxen: to use the new and more efficient plough, peasants pooled their oxen to form large plough-teams, originally receiving (it would appear) ploughed strips in proportion to their contribution. Thus, distribution of land was based no longer on the needs of a family but, rather, on the capacity of a power machine to till the earth. Man's relation to the soil was profoundly changed. Formerly man had been part of nature; now he was the exploiter of nature. Nowhere else in the world did farmers develop any analogous agricultural implement. Is it coincidence that modern technology, with its ruthlessness towards nature, has so largely been produced by descendants of these peasants of northern Europe?

This same exploitive attitude appears slightly before A.D. 830 in Western illustrated calendars. In older calendars the months were shown as passive personifications. The new Frankish calendars, which set the style for the Middle Ages, are very different: they show men coercing the world around them—ploughing, harvesting, chopping trees, butchering pigs. Man and nature are two things, and man is master.

These novelties seem to be in harmony with larger intellectual patterns. What people do about their ecology depends on what they think about themselves in relation to things around them. Human ecology is deeply conditioned by beliefs about our nature and destiny—that is, by religion. To Western eyes this is very evident in, say, India or Ceylon. It is equally true of ourselves and of our medieval ancestors.

The victory of Christianity over paganism was the greatest psychic revolution in the history of our culture. It has become fashionable today to say that, for better or worse, we live in 'the post-Christian age'. Certainly the forms of our thinking and language have largely ceased to be Christian, but to my eye the substance often remains amazingly akin to that of the past. Our daily habits of action, for example, are dominated by an implicit faith in perpetual progress which was unknown either to Græco-Roman antiquity or to the Orient. It is rooted in, and is indefensible apart from, Judeo-Christian teleology. The fact that Communists share it merely helps to show what can be demonstrated on many other grounds : that Marxism, like Islam, is a Judeo-Christian heresy. We continue today to live, as we have lived for about 1,700 years, very largely in a context of Christian axioms.

What did Christianity tell people about their relations with the environment?

While many of the world's mythologies provide stories of creation, Græco-Roman mythology was singularly incoherent in this respect. Like Aristotle, the intellectuals of the ancient West denied that the visible world had had a beginning. Indeed, the idea of a beginning was impossible in the framework of their cylical notion of time. In sharp contrast, Christianity inherited from Judaism not only a concept of time as non-repetitive and linear but also a striking story of creation. By gradual stages a loving and all-powerful God had created light and darkness, the heavenly bodies, the earth and all its plants, animals, birds and fishes. Finally, God had created Adam and, as an afterthought, Eve to keep man from being lonely. Man named all the animals, thus establishing his dominance over them. God planned all of this explicitly for man's benefit and rule : no item in the physical creation had any purpose save to serve man's purposes. And, although man's body is made of clay, he is not simply part of nature: he is made in God's image.

Especially in its Western form, Christianity is the most anthropocentric religion the world has seen. As early as the second century both Tertullian and Saint Irenæus of Lyons were insisting that when God shaped Adam he was foreshadowing the image of the incarnate Christ, the Second Adam. Man shares, in great measure, God's transcendence of nature. Christianity, in absolute contrast to ancient paganism and Asia's religions (except, perhaps, Zoroastrianism), not only established a dualism of man and nature but also insisted that it is God's will that man exploit nature for his proper ends.

At the level of the common people this worked out in an interesting way. In Antiquity every tree, every spring, every stream, every hill had its own *genius loci*, its guardian spirit. These spirits were accessible to men, but were very unlike men; centaurs, fauns and mermaids show their ambivalence. Before one cut a tree, mined a mountain, or dammed a brook, it was important to placate the spirit in charge of that particular situation, and to keep it placated. By destroying pagan animism, Christianity made it possible to exploit nature in a mood of indifference to the feelings of natural objects.

It is often said that for animism the Church substituted the cults of saints. True; but the cult of saints is functionally quite different from animism. The saint is not *in* natural objects; he may have special shrines, but his citizenship is in heaven. Moreover, a saint is entirely a man; he can be approached in human terms. In addition to saints, Christianity of course also had angels and demons inherited from Judaism and perhaps, at one remove, from Zoroastrianism. But these were all as mobile as the saints themselves. The spirits *in* natural objects, which formerly had protected nature from man, evaporated. Man's effective monopoly on spirit in this world was confirmed, and the old inhibitions to the exploitation of nature crumbled.

When one speaks in such sweeping terms, a note of caution is in order. Christianity is a complex faith, and its consequences differ in differing contexts. What I have said may well apply to the medieval West, where in fact technology made spectacular advances. But the Greek East, a highly civilised realm of equal Christian devotion, seems to have produced no marked technological innovation after the late seventh century, when Greek fire was invented. The key to the contrast may perhaps be found in a difference in the tonality of piety and thought which students of comparative theology find between the Greek and the Latin Churches. The Greeks believed that sin was intellectual blindness, and that salvation was found in illumination, orthodoxy—that is, clear thinking. The Latins, on the other hand, felt that sin was moral evil, and that salvation was to be found in right conduct. Eastern theology has been intellectualist. Western theology has been voluntarist. The Greek saint contemplates; the Western saint acts. The implications of Christianity for the conquest of nature would emerge more easily in the Western atmosphere.

The Christian dogma of creation, which is found in the first clause of all the Creeds, has another meaning for our comprehension of today's ecologic crisis. By revelation, God had given man the Bible, the Book of Scripture. But since God had made nature, nature also must reveal the divine mentality. The religious study of nature for the better understanding of God was known as natural theology. In the early Church, and always in the Greek East, nature was conceived primarily as a symbolic system through which God speaks to men: the ant is a sermon to sluggards; rising flames are the symbol of the soul's aspiration. This view of nature was essentially artistic rather than scientific. While Byzantium preserved and copied great numbers of ancient Greek scientific texts, science as we conceive it could scarcely flourish in such an ambience.

However, in the Latin West by the early thirteenth century natural theology was following a very different bent. It was ceasing to be the decoding of the physical symbols of God's communication with man and was becoming the effort to understand God's mind by discovering how his creation operates. The rainbow was no longer simply a symbol of hope first sent to Noah after the Deluge: Robert Grosseteste, Frair Roger Bacon and Theodoric of Freiberg produced startlingly sophisticated work on the optics of the rainbow, but they did it as a venture in religious understanding. From the thirteenth century onward, up to and including Leibnitz and Newton, every major scientist, in effect, explained his motivations in religious terms. Indeed, if Galileo had not been so expert an amateur theologian he would have got into far less trouble: the professionals resented his intrusion. And Newton seems to have regarded himself more as a theologian than as a scientist. It was not until the late eighteenth century that the hypothesis of God became unnecessary to many scientists.

It is often hard for the historian to judge, when men explain why they are doing what they want to do, whether they are offering real reasons or merely culturally acceptable reasons. The consistency with which scientists during the long formative centuries of Western science said that the task and the reward of the scientist was 'to think God's thoughts after him' leads one to believe that this was their real motivation. If so, then modern Western science was cast in a matrix of Christian theology. The dynamism of religious devotion, shaped by the Judeo-Christian dogma of creation, gave it impetus.

## An Alternative Christian View

We would seem to be headed towards conclusions unpalatable to many Christians. Since both *science* and *technology* are blessed words in our contemporary vocabulary, some may be happy at the notions, first, that, viewed historically, modern science is an extrapolation of natural theology and, second, that modern technology is at least partly to be explained as an Occidental, voluntarist realisation of the Christian dogma of man's transcendence of, and rightful mastery over, nature. But, as we now recognise, somewhat over a century ago science and technology—hitherto quite separate activities—joined to give mankind powers which, to judge by many of the ecologic effects, are out of control. If so, Christianity bears a huge burden of guilt.

I personally doubt that disastrous ecologic backlash can be avoided simply by applying to our problems more science and more technology. Our science and technology have grown out of Christian attitudes towards man's relation to nature which are almost universally held not only by Christians and neo-Christians but also by those who fondly regard themselves as post-Christians. Despite Copernicus, all the cosmos rotates around our little globe. Despite Darwin, we are *not*, in our hearts, part of the natural process. We are superior to nature, contemptuous of it, willing to use it for our slightest whim. The newly-elected Governor of California, like myself a churchman but less troubled than I, spoke for the Christian tradition when he said (as is alleged), 'when you've seen one redwood tree, you've seen them all'. To a Christian a tree can be no more than a physical fact. The whole concept of the sacred grove is alien to Christianity and to the ethos of the West. For nearly two millennia Christian missionaries have been chopping down sacred groves, which are idolatrous because they assume spirit in nature.

What we do about ecology depends on our ideas of the man–nature relationship. More science and more technology are not going to get us out of the present ecologic crisis until we find a new religion, or rethink our old one. The beatniks, who are the basic revolutionaries of our time, show a sound instinct in their affinity for Zen Buddhism, which conceives of the man–nature relationship as very nearly the mirror image of the Christian view. Zen, however, is as deeply conditioned by Asian history as Christianity is by the experience of the West, and I am dubious of its viability among us.

Possibly we should ponder the greatest radical in Christian history since Christ: St. Francis of Assisi. The prime miracle of St. Francis is the fact that he did not end at the stake, as many of his left-wing followers did. He was so clearly heretical that a General of the Franciscan Order, St. Bonaventura, a great and perceptive Christian, tried to suppress the early accounts of Franciscanism. The key to an understanding of Francis is his belief in the virtue of humility—not merely for the individual but for man as a species. Francis tried to depose man from his monarchy over creation and set up a democracy of all God's creatures. With him the ant is no longer simply a homily for the lazy, but is a sign of the thrust of the soul towards union with God; now they are Brother Ant and Sister Fire, praising the Creator in their own ways as Brother Man does in his.

Later commentators have said that Francis preached to the birds as a rebuke to men who would not listen. The records do not read so: he urged the little birds to praise God, and in spiritual ecstasy they flapped their wings and chirped rejoicing. Legends of saints, especially the Irish saints, had long told of their dealings with animals but always, I believe, to show their human dominance over creatures. With Francis it is different. The land around Gubbio in the Apennines was being ravaged by a fierce wolf. St. Francis, says the legend, talked to the wolf and persuaded him of the error of his ways. The wolf repented, died in the odour of sanctity and was buried in consecrated ground.

What Sir Steven Runciman calls 'the Franciscan doctrine of the animal soul' was quickly stamped out. Quite possibly it was in part inspired, consciously or unconsciously, by the belief in reincarnation held by the Cathar heretics who at that time teemed in Italy and southern France, and who presumably had got it originally from India. It is significant that at just the same moment, about 1200, traces of metempsychosis are found also in western Judaism, in the Provençal *Cabbala*. But Francis held neither to transmigration of souls nor to pantheism. His view of nature and of man rested on a unique sort of pan-psychism of all things animate and inanimate, designed for the glorification of their transcendent Creator, who, in the ultimate gesture of cosmic humility, assumed flesh, lay helpless in a manger, and hung dying on a scaffold.

I am not suggesting that many contemporary Americans who are concerned about our ecologic crisis will be either able or willing to counsel with wolves or exhort birds. However, the present increasing disruption of the global environment is the product of a dynamic technology and science which were originating in the Western medieval world against which St. Francis was rebelling in so original a way. Their growth cannot be understood historically apart from distinctive attitudes towards nature which are deeply grounded in Christian dogma. The fact that most people do not think of these attitudes as Christian is irrelevant. No new set of basic values has been accepted in our society to displace those of Christianity. Hence we shall continue to have a worsening ecologic crisis until we reject the Christian axiom that nature has no reason for existence save to serve man.

The greatest spiritual revolutionary in Western history, St. Francis, proposed what he thought was an alternative Christian view of nature and man's relation to it: he tried to substitute the idea of the equality of all creatures, including man, for the idea of man's limitless rule of creation. He failed. Both our present science and our present technology are so tinctured with orthodox Christian arrogance towards nature that no solution for our ecologic crisis can be expected from them alone. Since the roots of our trouble are so largely religious, the remedy must also be essentially religious, whether we call it that or not. We must rethink and refeel our nature and destiny. The profoundly religious, but heretical, sense of the primitive Franciscans for the spiritual autonomy of all parts of nature may point a direction. I propose Francis as a patron saint for ecologists.

## Appendix II

### Why Worry About Nature?
#### Richard L. Means[1]

Albert Schweitzer once wrote, 'The great fault of all ethics hitherto has been that they believed themselves to have to deal only with the relation of man to man.' Modern ethical discussion does not seem to have removed itself very far from this fallacy. Joseph Fletcher's *Situation Ethics: The New Morality*, for instance, deals piecemeal with man's relations to his fellows without even suggesting that man's relation to nature—to the physical and biological world—raises questions of moral behaviour. Perhaps this oversight is due to the general psychological and subjective tone of much current social criticism. Or, even more likely, it represents the 'revolt against formalism', the eschewing of the abstract and sweeping interpretations of man and nature once the passion of American social scientists.

It is true that the Thoreau-like comments of Joseph Wood Krutch or the aggressive naturalistic interpretations of the Austrian scientist, Konrad Lorenz, find a grudging response among some social scientists. But contemporary social scientists have so completely separated considerations of culture from nature that it will take some intellectual effort to overcome this dichotomy. Moreover, although the relations of man and nature may be envisioned in various ways—all the way from control to passive obedience—the notion that man's relation to nature is a moral one finds very few articulate champions, even among contemporary religious writers. Har-

[1] Richard L. Means is associate professor of sociology at Kalamazoo (Michigan) College.

vey Cox's book, *The Secular City*, for example, is set in an urban world in rather extreme isolation from the surrounding problems of resources, food, disease, etc. The city is taken for granted and the moral dimensions of Cox's analysis are limited to man's relations to man within this urban world, and not with the animals, the plants, the trees, the air—that is, the natural habitat.

Eric Hoffer, one of the few contemporary social critics who have met head-on the issue of man's relationship to nature, has warned in these pages of the danger of romanticising nature. ['A Strategy for the War with Nature,' *SR*, February 5, 1966.] Longshoreman, dishwasher, student of human tragedy and exposer of the corruptions and perversions of power, Mr. Hoffer says that the great accomplishment of man is to transcend nature, to separate one's self from the demands of the instinct. Thus, according to Hoffer, a fundamental characteristic of man is to be found in his capacity to free himself from the restrictions of the physical and biological.

In a way, Hoffer is correct. Surely the effects on man of flood, famine, fire and earthquake have been great and hardly indicate a beneficence in nature which is ready and willing to rush headlong to the succour of man. But Hoffer's attack is basically political. It is an attack on 'romantic individualism'—a special interpretation of man's relation to nature. Hoffer knows full well that romantic individualism leads easily to a kind of egoism and anti-rationalism which can pervert and destroy democratic institutions.

One is reminded of Hitler's call to neglect reason and to 'think with one's blood'. Values—tradition, home soil, nationalism and race—have often been legitimised on the basis of a vague nature mysticism. Such a nature mysticism is the very essence of romantic individualism (though, of course, there may be other types of nature romanticism which do not advocate egotist striving). Perhaps the problem lies in the focus on the 'individual' as delineated by Hoffer. He assumes that the response to nature couched in the terms of a naïve faith in nature's bountiful, miracle-working properties is an individual response. And, of course, it always is, to a degree, but by failure to consider the collective or social side of man's relation to nature, the true moral dimensions of the problem are obscured.

It may be that *man* is at war with nature, but *men* are not (or, at least, cannot be). The reason is that certain individual attitudes and actions, when taken collectively, have consequences for nature, and these consequences may be most clearly understood under the stark realities of social survival itself. Take the problems of radioactive wastes, Strontium 90 contamination, etc. Man does not just do battle with the natural world; he may, in the act of co-operating with it, also shape and change it. Men join in a chain of decisions which facilitate the emergence of a new symbiotic relationship to nature—that is, we create civilisation and culture. This crucial assumption strikes at the very roots of romantic individualism. One man, totally alone, acting before nature and using nature to satisfy needs of warmth, comfort and creativity, is very difficult to imagine. Even Robinson Crusoe had his Man Friday!

Hoffer seems to neglect the possibility that man's co-operation in the subjection of nature need not be conceptualised simply on the basis of brute force. Physical work, mechanical and otherwise—from the labour of the Chinese masses to the works of a sophisticated high-tower steeplejack—depends on the intrusion of human ideas into the natural world. Aided by machines, cranes, bulldozers, factories, transportation systems, computers and laboratories, man does force nature's hand. This does not, however, force us to an acceptance of metaphysical materialism, the naïve belief that matter and physical force are the only realities. The power of ideas, of values, provides the presuppositions which in the first place create a particular web of human interaction between nature and man. The power of the contemplative idea, the chain of speculative reason, the mathematician's art and the philosopher's dreams must also be considered. If this point of view is accepted, then the question of man's relation to nature is a much more crucial moral issue that Eric Hoffer seems to suggest.

What, then, is the moral crisis? It is, I think, a pragmatic problem—that is, it involves the actual social consequences of myriad and unconnected acts. The crisis comes from the combined results of a mistreatment of our environment. It involves the negligence of a small businessman on the Kalamazoo River, the irresponsibility of a large corporation on Lake Erie, the impatient use of insecticides by a farmer in California, the stripping of land by Kentucky mine operators. Unfortunately, there is a long history of unnecessary and tragic destruction of animal and natural resources on the face of this continent.

One might begin the indictment with the classical case of the passenger pigeon which once flew across America in tremendous numbers, and then end with the destruction of the seal industry. The trouble is, however, we do not seem to learn very much from these sad happenings, for (to the anguish of men who have thrilled to the images created by Herman Melville and the great white whale) such marine scientists as Scott McVay believe that commercial fishing is endangering the whale, the last abundant species in the world. For those more inclined towards a cash nexus, there goes a profitable industry. For those of us who have a respect for nature—in particular, for our mammalian kinsmen—the death of these great creatures will leave a void in God's creation and in the imagination of men for generations to come.

Another case in point is the attempt to dam and flood mile after mile of the Grand Canyon in order to produce more electricity—a commodity we seem to have in great abundance. The Grand Canyon, of course, is not a commodity; it is truly, in popular parlance, a 'happening'. Uncontrolled by man, created by nature, it cannot be duplicated. Any assault on its natural state is an equal attack on man's capacity to wonder, to contemplate his environment and nature's work. In short, such activities seem to belittle and diminish man himself. Thus the activities of those who suggest such destruction assume a restricted view of man and his capacity for joy in nature. In this sense, such activities are immoral. We could lengthen the list, but it should be clear that destruction of nature by man's gratuitous 'busyness' and technological arrogance is the result of a thoughtless and mindless human activity.

A second basic issue is the growing biological pollution of the environment. Discussions of the pollution in just one river, the mighty Hudson, in financial terms stagger the imagination. The economic costs just to keep the river in its present undesirable state are immense—and to make any progress back towards a less polluted river will cost billions of dollars. The same is true of other great bodies of water.

And consider the state of the air we breathe. Air pollution has demonstrable ill effects on man, as many reports confirm. But in addition, for the economically minded, A. J. Haagen-Smit, a leading expert on air pollution, notes that a largely ignored breakdown in standards of efficiency and technology also is involved:

From all the emissions of an automobile, the total loss of fuel energy is about 15 per cent; in the U.S. that represents a loss of about $3 billion annually. It is remarkable that the automobile industry, which has a reputation for efficiency, allows such fuel waste.

Perhaps an issue becomes most moral when it is personal, existential—appeals to our own experience. Scientists vary in estimates of the time when the Great Lakes will be largely polluted, but the day of reckoning may be much too near. When I was a boy in Toledo, Ohio, summer after summer many of my neighbours and playmates went to cottages along the shores of Lake Erie. Today, visiting these cottages is anything but a happy event, and some owners are attempting desperately to sell their properties to any bidder. An analysis by Charles F. Powers and Andrew Robertson on 'The Aging Great Lakes' [*Scientific American,* November 1966] is not at all comforting for those of us who love the miles of sandy beach of Lake Michigan or the rugged, cold, windwhipped shores of Lake Superior. Although Lake Michigan will not immediately turn into a polluted wasteland like Lake Erie, with dark spots of water without aeration where only worms can live, pollution is growing in the southern end of Lake Michigan. And these problems, as Powers and Robertson point out, are beginning to touch even relatively unspoiled Lake Superior.

Why is man's relation to nature a moral crisis? It is a moral crisis because it is a historical one involving man's history and culture, expressed at its roots by our religious and ethical views of nature—which have been relatively unquestioned in this context. The historian of medieval culture, Lynn White, Jr., brilliantly traced the origin and consequences of this expression in an insightful article in *Science* last March: 'The Historical Roots of Our Ecologic Crisis.' He argues that the Christian notion of a transcendent God, removed from nature and breaking into nature only through revelation, removed spirit from nature and allows, in the ideological sense, for an easy exploitation of nature.

On the American scene, the Calvinistic and the deistic concepts of God were peculiarly alike at this point.

Both envisioned God as absolutely transcendent, apart from the world, isolated from nature and organic life. As to the contemporary implications of this dichotomy between spirit and nature, Professor White says:

> The newly-elected Governor of California, like myself a churchman but less troubled than I, spoke for the Christian tradition when he said (as is alleged), 'when you've seen one redwood tree, you've seen them all'. To a Christian a tree can be no more than a physical fact. The whole concept of the sacred grove is alien to Christianity and to the ethos of the West. For nearly two millennia Christian missionaries have been chopping down sacred groves, which are idolatrous because they assume spirit in nature.

Perhaps, as Lynn White suggests, the persistence of this as a moral problem is illustrated in the protest of the contemporary generation of beats and hippies. Although the kind of 'cool cat' aloofness expressed by this generation grates on the nerves of many of us, and more than a few 'squares' find difficulty in 'digging' the new hair styles (not to mention Twiggy), there may be a 'sound instinct' involved in the fact that some of these so-called beats have turned to Zen Buddhism. It may represent an overdue perception of the fact that we need to appreciate more fully the religious and moral dimensions of the relation between nature and the human spirit.

Why do almost all of our wisest and most exciting social critics meticulously avoid the moral implications of this issue? Perhaps, in the name of political realism, it is too easy to fear the charge that one anthropomorphises or spiritualises nature. On the other hand, the refusal to connect the human spirit to nature may reflect the traditional thought pattern of Western society wherein nature is conceived to be a separate substance—a material—

mechanical, and, in a metaphysical sense, irrelevant to man.

It seems to me much more fruitful to think of nature as part of a system of human organisation—as a variable, a changing condition—which interacts with man and culture. If nature is to perceived, then a love, a sense of awe and a feeling of empathy with nature need not degenerate into a subjective, emotional bid for romantic individualism. On the contrary, such a view should help destroy egoistic, status politics, for it helps unmask the fact that other men's activities are not just private, inconsequential and limited in themselves; their acts, mediated through changes in nature, affect my life, my children and the generations to come. In this sense, justification of a technological arrogance towards nature on the basis of dividends and profits is not just bad economics—it is basically an immoral act. And our contemporary moral crisis, then, goes much deeper than questions of political power and law, of urban riots and slums. It may, at least in part, reflect American society's almost utter disregard for the value of nature.